I0426259

July 2012

SECURE COMMUNITIES

Criminal Alien Removals Increased, but Technology Planning Improvements Needed

GAO

Accountability ★ Integrity ★ Reliability

Highlights

Highlights of GAO-12-708, a report to the Ranking Member, Committee on Homeland Security, House of Representatives

SECURE COMMUNITIES

Criminal Alien Removals Increased, but Technology Planning Improvements Needed

Why GAO Did This Study

Initiated in 2008, Secure Communities is an ICE program designed to identify potentially removable aliens, particularly those with criminal convictions, in state and local law enforcement custody. Fingerprints checked against a Federal Bureau of Investigation criminal database are checked against DHS's immigration database to help determine whether an arrested individual is removable. GAO was asked to review Secure Communities operations. This report addresses (1) enforcement trends under Secure Communities, (2) ICE's adherence to best practices in acquiring Secure Communities–related technology, and (3) ICE safeguards to help protect against potential civil rights abuses under Secure Communities. GAO analyzed ICE data on removals from October 2008 through March 2012, and arrest charges from October 2010 through March 2012; reviewed program guidance, policies, and reports; and interviewed ICE's Law Enforcement Support Center and agency officials, local law enforcement and community groups in four locations selected for geographic diversity, among other factors. These perspectives are not generalizable, but provided insights into Secure Communities operations.

What GAO Recommends

GAO recommends that ICE develop well-defined requirements and an integrated master schedule that accounts for all activities for its technology contracts, and a plan for workforce changes in preparation for full technology deployment. DHS concurred with the recommendations.

View GAO-12-708. For more information, contact Rebecca Gambler at (202) 512-8777 or gamblerr@gao.gov.

What GAO Found

Data from the Department of Homeland Security's (DHS) Immigration and Customs Enforcement (ICE) indicate that the percentage of its removals attributable to Secure Communities increased from about 4 percent in fiscal year 2009 to about 20 percent in fiscal year 2011. Of about 183,000 aliens removed under the program from October 2008 through March 2012, about 74 percent had a criminal conviction. ICE did not have state or local arrest charges for about 56 percent of alien Secure Communities removals from October 2010 (when ICE began collecting arrest charges) through March 2012, so we were unable to determine the most frequent arrest charges under the program. For the 44 percent of aliens removed on whom ICE collected arrest charge data, traffic offenses, including driving under the influence of alcohol, were the most frequent arrest charges. ICE is taking steps to improve the collection of arrest charge data, but it is too early to assess the effectiveness of its efforts.

ICE has not consistently followed best practices in acquiring technology to help determine the immigration status of aliens identified by Secure Communities. ICE awarded contracts to modernize its technology without fully defining requirements or developing an integrated master schedule—two best practices for managing capital programs. As a result, ICE encountered delays, cost increases, and products that did not meet ICE's needs. For example, ICE spent $14.3 million for one contract to develop services that ICE found to be unusable. Establishing well-defined requirements and developing an integrated schedule for completing technology modernization could better position ICE to prevent delays and cost increases. Further, ICE plans to develop a workforce plan after the systems are deployed. Developing a workforce plan prior to full system deployment, consistent with internal controls, could better position ICE to effectively use staff when it deploys the modernized technology.

DHS's Office of Civil Rights and ICE identified four safeguards to help protect aliens' civil rights under Secure Communities, including providing detainees with a revised detainer form with telephone numbers to call when they feel their civil rights have been violated. Officials are also developing briefing materials on how to protect aliens' civil rights, statistically analyzing arrest and other information to identify potential civil rights abuses, and using an existing DHS complaint process for addressing Secure Communities concerns.

Number and Percentage of ICE's Removals Attributed to Secure Communities, by Fiscal Year

Year	ICE removals	Removals attributed to Secure Communities	Percentage of ICE removals attributed to Secure Communities
2009	389,834	14,363	4
2010	392,862	49,498	13
2011	396,606	79,876	20
2012: October 2011 through March 2012	187,763	39,159	21
Total	1,367,065	182,896	13

Source: GAO analysis of data provided by ICE.

Contents

Letter   1

    Background   6
    Most Secure Communities Removals Were Criminal Aliens, but
      Arrest Charge Data Are Incomplete   14
    ICE Is Modernizing Its Technology System for Determining
      Immigration Status, but Acquisition and Implementation
      Planning Could Be Improved   24
    ICE and CRCL Identified Safeguards to Help Address Potential
      Civil Rights Abuses under Secure Communities; Some Efforts
      Have Not Yet Been Fully Implemented   35
    Conclusions   44
    Recommendations for Executive Action   44
    Agency Comments and GAO's Evaluation   45

Appendix I   Alien Criminal Response Information Management Modernization
    Contracts   47

Appendix II   Comments from the Department of Homeland Security   50

Appendix III   GAO Contacts and Staff Acknowledgments   53

Tables

    Table 1: ICE's Civil Immigration Enforcement Removal Priorities   10
    Table 2: Number and Percentage of ICE's Removals Attributed to
      Secure Communities, by Fiscal Year   15
    Table 3: Arrest Charge Information for Aliens That Secure
      Communities Identified and ICE Removed during Fiscal
      Year 2011 and the First Half of Fiscal Year 2012, Including
      the Most Frequent Arrest Charge Categories   23
    Table 4: ACRIMe Modernization Projects   26
    Table 5: Comparison of Schedule and Cost Estimates   27
    Table 6: ACRIMe Modernization Contracts   47

Figures

Figure 1: The Secure Communities Process   9
Figure 2: Secure Communities Activation Status as of June 5, 2012   13
Figure 3: Classification of 182,896 Aliens Who Were Removed by
          ICE after Being Identified by Secure Communities from
          October 2008 through March 2012   17
Figure 4: Arrest Locations of Aliens Identified by Secure
          Communities and Removed by ICE, From October 2008
          through March 2012   19
Figure 5: Composition of Secure Communities Removals by Fiscal
          Year   21
Figure 6: Detainer Form Notice to Detainee   36

Abbreviations

ACRIMe	Alien Criminal Response Information Management
ATP	Automated Threat Prioritization
CAP	Criminal Alien Program
CBP	Customs and Border Protection
CRCL	Office for Civil Rights and Civil Liberties
DHS	Department of Homeland Security
ERO	Enforcement and Removal Operations
EWI	entry without inspection
FBI	Federal Bureau of Investigation
IAFIS	Integrated Automated Fingerprint Identification System
IAQ	Immigration Alien Query
ICE	Immigration and Customs Enforcement
IDENT	Automated Biometric Identification System
IRC	Interoperability Response Center
LEA	law enforcement agency
LESC	Law Enforcement Support Center
NIBRS	National Incident-Based Reporting System
NCIC	National Crime Information Center
OIG	Office of the Inspector General
OPR	Office of Professional Responsibility
SDS	Status Determination Support
UCR	Uniform Crime Reporting
YTD	year to date

United States Government Accountability Office
Washington, DC 20548

July 13, 2012

The Honorable Bennie Thompson
Ranking Member
Committee on Homeland Security
House of Representatives

Dear Mr. Thompson:

The Department of Homeland Security (DHS) estimated that as of January 2011 there were about 11.5 million aliens (non-U.S. citizens) living in the United States without lawful immigration status.[1] DHS's U.S. Immigration and Customs Enforcement (ICE) is responsible for apprehending and removing aliens who have violated immigration law. All aliens not lawfully present in the United States are potentially removable. Removal is a civil enforcement process that does not lead to a criminal conviction.[2] A criminal alien is a noncitizen in the United States, who may be present on a lawful basis or not, who has been convicted of a crime. A criminal alien lawfully in the United States may be removable, depending on the nature of the particular offense of which the alien was convicted.[3] Secure Communities, initiated in 2008 and expected by DHS to be deployed nationwide by 2013, is one of ICE's programs for identifying potentially removable aliens arrested by state or local law enforcement agencies, particularly those with criminal convictions. Under Secure Communities, the fingerprints that these agencies submit to the Department of Justice's Federal Bureau of Investigation (FBI) for criminal background checks are automatically forwarded to DHS for comparison with fingerprint records DHS maintains. If the fingerprints match DHS's records, ICE is to use its information systems to access law enforcement and immigration databases to conduct additional analysis of the

---

[1] See DHS, *Estimates of the Unauthorized Immigrant Population Residing in the United States: January 2011*, Office of Immigration Statistics Policy Directorate, March 2012.

[2] Aliens who are subject to removal for violating immigration law may be prosecuted criminally as well. For example, it is a criminal offense to enter or attempt to enter the United States at a time or place other than as designated by immigration officers or to enter the United States after having been removed from the country. See 8 U.S.C. §§ 1325, 1326.

[3] See 8 U.S.C. § 1227(a)(2) for descriptions of criminal offenses that make any alien removable.

individuals' immigration status and criminal history, and determine whether to request that the law enforcement agency hold the subject so ICE can take custody for further enforcement action.

Secure Communities is one of four programs under ICE to identify criminal aliens who are subject to removal, a key agency enforcement priority. In addition to Secure Communities, ICE's Criminal Alien Program (CAP) is designed to identify, process, and remove criminal aliens from prisons across the United States; the National Fugitive Operations Program is to pursue known at-large criminal aliens and fugitive aliens; and the 287(g) program, authorized by section 287(g) of the Immigration and Nationality Act,[4] is to provide state and local law enforcement agency officers with delegation of authority, training, and resources to perform certain functions of an immigration officer.[5] While identifying criminal aliens is a priority for ICE, individuals identified by Secure Communities who are not convicted for the offense for which they are arrested and have no previous criminal conviction may be removed because they fall under other ICE priorities (such as previous violations of immigration laws).[6]

Different stakeholders have provided differing perspectives on the effects of Secure Communities. According to ICE, Secure Communities strengthens public safety by improving ICE's ability to identify, detain, and ultimately remove criminal aliens nationwide. ICE has also reported that Secure Communities reduces the potential for racial or ethnic profiling by state and local law enforcement agencies because anyone who is arrested and fingerprinted is subject to the Secure Communities matching process. In contrast, some immigrant advocacy groups have expressed concern that the program encourages racial profiling because officers

---

[4]See 8 U.S.C. § 1357(g).

[5]In 2009 GAO reported that the 287(g) program lacked documented objectives and some community members raised concerns about potential misuse of the program. GAO recommended and ICE agreed to document the 287(g) program objective, document and communicate supervisory activities, and specify data each agency is to collect and report. DHS has since implemented these recommendations. See GAO, *Immigration Enforcement: Better Controls Needed over Program Authorizing State and Local Enforcement of Federal Immigration Laws*, GAO-09-109 (Washington, D.C: Jan. 30, 2009).

[6]Other ICE criminal alien–targeted programs may also identify aliens who are removable but have not been convicted of crimes.

could find pretexts to arrest individuals based on their physical appearance, knowing that they will be screened for immigration status as a result of the arrest. Further, these groups believe that Secure Communities discourages witnesses of crimes and domestic violence victims from contacting law enforcement for fear of possible deportation. A DHS Advisory Task Force identified similar community concerns, based in part on forums held in communities across the country, and concluded that such fears could erode the police's ability to build strong relationships with immigrant communities and engage in community policing.[7]

In March and April 2012, DHS's Office of Inspector General issued two reports on Secure Communities, one of which reviewed how ICE communicated the intent and requirements for participation in Secure Communities to states and local jurisdictions, and the other reviewed ICE's operation of Secure Communities.[8] ICE agreed with recommendations made in both reports.

You asked us to review ICE's implementation of the Secure Communities program. This report addresses the following questions: (1) What trends can be identified in ICE's enforcement actions related to the Secure Communities program? (2) To what extent has ICE adhered to best practices to acquire Secure Communities–related technology? (3) What safeguards, if any, does ICE have in place to protect against potential civil rights abuses under Secure Communities?

To address these objectives, we conducted five site visits. Four visits were to ICE field offices in Washington, D.C.; Los Angeles, California;

---

[7]Homeland Security Advisory Council, *Task Force on Secure Communities Findings and Recommendations*, September 2011. In its response to the task force's findings and recommendations, ICE, among other things, clarified its enforcement policy related to minor traffic violations. For individuals arrested solely for minor traffic offenses, who have not previously been convicted of other crimes and do not fall within any other ICE priority category, ICE said it will only consider making a detainer operative upon conviction for the minor criminal traffic offense. Minor traffic offenses do not include driving under the influence of alcohol, hit-and-run, reckless driving resulting in injury to persons, or other violations that have the potential for causing serious injury or harm to the public. (ICE, *Protecting the Homeland: ICE Response to the Task Force on Secure Communities Findings and Recommendations*, Apr. 27, 2012.)

[8]DHS, Office of the Inspector General, *Communication Regarding Participation in Secure Communities*, OIG-12-66 (Washington, D.C.: March 2012), and *Operations of United States Immigration and Customs Enforcement's Secure Communities*, OIG-12-64 (Washington, D.C.: April 2012) (Revised).

Chicago, Illinois; and Miami, Florida, where we met with agency officials, local law enforcement officials, and community groups. We selected these field offices because they are geographically dispersed and would provide perspectives from different parts of the country, and because the Los Angeles, Chicago, and Miami field offices house three of ICE's four Interoperability Response Centers where Secure Communities fingerprint match information is analyzed. The information obtained from these visits is not generalizable to other ICE field offices, but it provided valuable insights into Secure Communities implementation. We also visited ICE's Law Enforcement Support Center (LESC) in Williston, Vermont, where we met with officials responsible for determining the immigration status of individuals identified by Secure Communities as potentially removable.

To identify trends in ICE's enforcement actions related to the Secure Communities program, we reviewed ICE's progress reports for activating jurisdictions into the program and conducted interviews with ICE officials on each of our site visits. We reviewed ICE alien removal data from October 2008 through March 2012, and analyzed arrest charges for aliens removed from the United States during fiscal year 2011, when ICE began collecting arrest charge data, and the first half of fiscal year 2012. We also examined ICE's policies and procedures for identifying and removing criminal aliens, and documents related to enforcement actions and detainers. We interviewed officials from ICE's Secure Communities and Law Enforcement Systems and Analysis offices. We assessed the reliability of Secure Communities–related data by examining documentation about the various systems that ICE uses to analyze Secure Communities fingerprint submissions and maintain information on aliens it encounters, and confirming with ICE officials that the documentation is accurate and up to date. In doing so, we confirmed that ICE has controls in place to ensure that the data it maintains on aliens encountered by the program are entered accurately. We determined that the data were sufficiently reliable for the purposes of this report.

To examine ICE's efforts to plan and manage the acquisition of technology for determining the immigration status of aliens identified through Secure Communities, we reviewed documents, such as contracts, acquisition plans, and project schedules, from 2007 through 2012, which corresponds to the time frame of ICE's acquisition efforts. We reviewed ICE workforce documents related to Secure Communities technologies, such as LESC budget and staffing data and ICE's Deployment Dashboard, a document listing each location where Secure Communities is activated or is planned to be activated. To obtain information on workload and staffing issues associated with planned technology changes, we interviewed headquarters officials in ICE's Enforcement and Removal Operations, officials responsible for overseeing technology procurements in ICE's Office of the Chief Information Officer and Office of Acquisition Management, and knowledgeable officials in the field offices we visited. We evaluated ICE's plans for acquiring a modernized system for determining the immigration status of Secure Communities matches using GAO's *Standards for Internal Control in the Federal Government*, and best practices for managing capital investments.[9]

To determine the extent to which DHS has safeguards in place to protect against potential civil rights abuses, we reviewed ICE documents, such as the detainer form—the form that ICE sends to state and local law enforcement agencies to request that they maintain custody of a removable alien—met with community groups at each of our site visits regarding Secure Communities, interviewed ICE officials responsible for managing the Secure Communities program, and officials in DHS's Office for Civil Rights and Civil Liberties (CRCL) responsible for addressing complaints and conducting monitoring activities related to Secure Communities. We viewed training videos CRCL developed for state and local law enforcement officials, and reviewed CRCL's dissemination and completion plans for additional training videos. We examined documents and discussed the status of CRCL's plans for monitoring arrests by state and local law enforcement with CRCL's statistician. We discussed CRCL's process for individuals to submit civil rights and civil liberties complaints associated with Secure Communities, and obtained summaries of complaint investigations under way. We reviewed LESC's summary statistics for calls received on its detainee phone line from December 26, 2011(when it was initiated), through April 17, 2012. We also reviewed examples of call records from January, February, and March 2012, and picked three for illustrative purposes. The examples are not generalizable, but provided us with perspectives on the types of calls LESC receives. To assess the reliability of the call record data, we discussed the call receipt process with LESC officials, reviewed the

---

[9]See GAO, *GAO Cost Estimating and Assessment Guide: Best Practices for Developing and Managing Capital Program Costs*, GAO-09-3SP (Washington, D.C.: March 2009); *Defense Acquisitions: A Knowledge-Based Funding Approach Could Improve Major Weapon System Program Outcomes*, GAO-08-619 (Washington, D.C.: July 2, 2008); *Standards for Internal Control in the Federal Government*, GAO/AIMD-00-21.3.1 (Washington, D.C: Nov. 1, 1999); and the Project Management Institute's *The Standard for Program Management* (Newton Square, PA © 2006).

relevant standard operating procedures, and reviewed the detainee phone line call categorization guidelines. We determined that the data were sufficiently reliable for our purposes.

We conducted this performance audit from July 2011 through July 2012, in accordance with generally accepted government auditing standards. Those standards require that we plan and perform the audit to obtain sufficient, appropriate evidence to provide a reasonable basis for our findings and conclusions based on our audit objectives. We believe that the evidence obtained provides a reasonable basis for our findings and conclusions based on our audit objectives.

Background

ICE has received funding specifically designated for removing criminal aliens. For example, the fiscal year 2008 DHS appropriations act made $200 million of ICE's salaries and expenses appropriation available through the end of fiscal year 2009 to "improve and modernize efforts to identify aliens convicted of a crime, sentenced to imprisonment, and who may be deportable, and remove them from the United States, once they are judged deportable."[10] In response, ICE initiated Secure Communities and issued a plan that detailed how ICE would implement policies and modernize technologies to accomplish its overall goal of identifying and removing criminal aliens.[11] ICE's Enforcement and Removal Operations (ERO) is responsible for identifying and apprehending removable aliens, detaining these individuals when it deems it necessary, and removing

---

[10]Consolidated Appropriations Act, 2008, Pub. L. No. 110-161, 121 Stat. 1844, 2050 (2007). DHS's fiscal year 2009 appropriations act specified that not less than $1 billion was available for identifying and removing criminal aliens, including $150 million to be available until the end of fiscal year 2010, and directed DHS to "prioritize the identification and removal of aliens convicted of a crime by the severity of that crime." Consolidated Security, Disaster Assistance, and Continuing Appropriations Act, 2009, Pub. L. No. 110-329, 122 Stat. 3574, 3659 (2008). In each of fiscal years 2010, 2011, and 2012, DHS's appropriations acts made almost $200 million of the funds directed to criminal alien enforcement available to ICE, and ICE allocated these funds to Secure Communities. See Pub. L. No. 111-83, 123 Stat. 2142, 2149 (2009); Pub. L. No. 112-10, 125 Stat. 38, 102-03, 140-41 (2011); Pub. L. No. 112-74, 125 Stat. 786, 949 (2011).

[11]The term "Secure Communities" is used to refer to ICE's comprehensive plan to identify and remove criminal aliens (which includes detention facilities, transportation, and other aspects of the overall process). The term is also used to refer to a component of the Secure Communities comprehensive plan that focuses on using technology to improve the identification of removable criminal aliens.

them from the United States. ERO manages the Secure Communities program and has 24 field offices nationwide.

Under Secure Communities, when an individual is arrested by a state or local law enforcement agency, the individual's fingerprints are taken and automatically checked against the Integrated Automated Fingerprint Identification System (IAFIS), a national fingerprint and criminal history system maintained by the FBI, and DHS's Automated Biometric Identification System (IDENT) to identify a fingerprint match.[12] IDENT contains fingerprint and other biometric information on immigration violators, known or suspected terrorists, criminal aliens, and foreign nationals who are enrolled in DHS's United States Visitor and Immigrant Status Indicator Technology program, among others.[13] When a law enforcement agency (LEA) arrests and books an individual on suspicion of committing a crime, the person's fingerprints are routinely sent to the FBI for a criminal background check. FBI electronically forwards the fingerprints to DHS for a check against IDENT records. If there is a fingerprint match, ICE is to then determine whether the individual is subject to removal.[14] On the basis of the match, the FBI is to send an Immigration Alien Query to ICE's LESC.[15] Using the Alien Criminal Response Information Management (ACRIMe) system, LESC specialists are to search multiple databases, such as the FBI's National Crime Information Center (NCIC) and the Student and Exchange Visitor Information System for information on the individual's criminal history and

---

[12]ICE labels this federal information sharing capability as IDENT/IAFIS interoperability. ICE's Secure Communities program uses interoperability between these two systems to identify potentially removable aliens. For the purposes of this report, we use the term "Secure Communities" when referring to Secure Communities' use of IDENT/IAFIS interoperability.

[13]DHS, in coordination with the Department of State, established the enrollment program to use biometric and biographic information to control and monitor the pre-entry, entry, status, and exit of certain foreign visitors and immigrants.

[14]Secure Communities does not identify all potentially removable aliens who are arrested because the IDENT database does not contain the fingerprints of all aliens; for example, aliens who cross the U.S. border illegally might not have their fingerprints in IDENT if they were never encountered by the Border Patrol or ICE. ICE is reviewing the results of a pilot to identify ways of determining the immigration status of arrested individuals whose fingerprints are not included in IDENT.

[15]LESC provides immigration status and identity information and real-time assistance to local, state, and federal law enforcement agencies on aliens suspected, arrested or convicted of criminal activity, among other things.

immigration status.[16] LESC is to then send an Immigration Alien Response to the LEA and relevant ICE ERO field office or Interoperability Response Center (IRC)—offices established in the Los Angeles, Chicago, Miami, and Buffalo, New York, field offices to expand ICE's ability to respond to Secure Communities matches.[17]

The ICE field office or response center is to then determine whether to send an immigration detainer (Form I-247) to the LEA that has custody of the individual.[18] A detainer is an ICE request that the law enforcement agency maintain custody of the individual for up to 48 hours after that person would otherwise be released, excluding weekends and holidays, to allow ICE time to administratively arrest (i.e., assume custody of) the person. The decision whether to issue a detainer for a particular alien is based on whether the alien falls within ICE's priorities for removal and other factors, such as whether ICE detention resources are available, and whether the individual is still in the custody of the arresting local or state law enforcement agency (under some circumstances a person may be held for only a few hours). If the individual is convicted and serves a criminal sentence, ICE is to wait until the sentence is completed to take the person into custody. Figure 1 describes the Secure Communities process.

---

[16]ACRIMe is an information system used by ICE to receive and respond to immigration status inquiries from federal, state, and local law enforcement agencies about individuals arrested, subject to background checks, or otherwise encountered by those agencies.

[17]IRCs process Secure Communities responses for their own field offices. During evening hours, IRCs also process responses for other field offices that do not have 24 hour/7day a week capabilities. The IRCs are staffed, in part, by contractors who review LESC's determination responses and by ICE agents who make detainer decisions.

[18]ICE also requests that law enforcement officials provide the subject with a copy of the detainer.

Figure 1: The Secure Communities Process

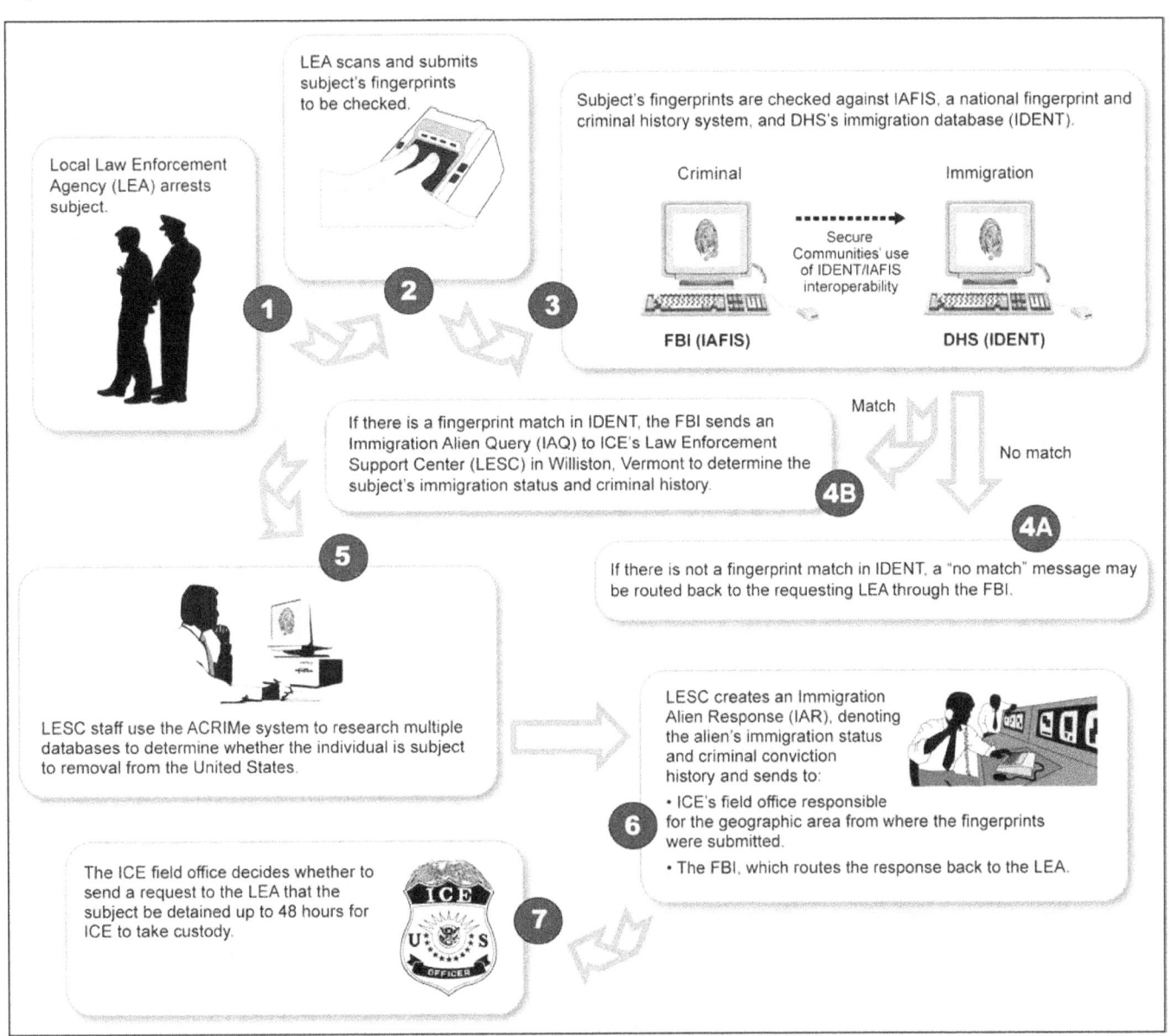

Source: GAO analysis of information provided by ICE.

According to ICE, Secure Communities helps carry out ICE's civil immigration enforcement priorities. In a March 2011 memorandum, ICE's Director provided guidance to all ICE employees on ICE's civil immigration enforcement priorities as they relate to the apprehension, detention, and removal of aliens across all ICE programs.[19] The types of crimes included under the different priority classifications are described in table 1.

Table 1: ICE's Civil Immigration Enforcement Removal Priorities

Priority	Priority description	
1	The removal of aliens who pose a danger to national security or public safety, including aliens convicted of crimes, with an emphasis on violent criminals, felons, and repeat offenders. Convicted criminal aliens (as a subset of Priority 1) are further prioritized into 3 levels based on their criminal conviction history.[a]	
		Examples of types of crimes
	Convicted Criminal Level 1: Includes aliens convicted of "aggravated felonies," as defined in § 101(a)(43) of the Immigration and Nationality Act, or two or more crimes punishable by more than one year, commonly referred to as felonies[b]	Homicide Kidnapping Rape Robbery Aggravated assault Sexual exploitation of a minor
	Convicted Criminal Level 2: Includes aliens convicted of any felony or three or more offenses punishable by less than 1 year, commonly referred to as misdemeanors	Manslaughter Extortion Vehicle theft Bribery Sex offenses (not involving assault or commercialized sex)
	Convicted Criminal Level 3: Includes aliens convicted of offenses punishable by less than 1 year	Simple Assault Driving Under the Influence Obstructing justice Drug possession Property crimes
2	The removal of aliens who have recently violated immigration controls at the border, at ports of entry or through the knowing abuse of visa programs.	
3	The removal of aliens who are fugitives or have otherwise obstructed immigration controls. It includes aliens who reenter the country illegally after removal or enter fraudulently.	

Source: GAO analysis of ICE information.

[a]Prior to fiscal year 2009, ICE did not categorize convicted criminal aliens by offense levels.

[b]"Aggravated felonies" under § 101(a)(43) of the Immigration and Nationality Act (8 U.S.C. § 1101(a)(43)) include various state and federal offenses ranging from murder, rape, and trafficking in controlled substances to theft, bribery, and obstruction of justice.

In a June 2011 memorandum, ICE's Director provided guidance to ICE officers, agents, and attorneys on the exercise of "prosecutorial

[19]ICE, *Civil Immigration Enforcement: Priorities for the Apprehension, Detention, and Removal of Aliens*, (Washington, D.C.: March 2, 2011).

discretion" to ensure that the agency's immigration enforcement resources are focused on its enforcement priorities.[20] As noted in the memorandum, because the agency is confronted with more administrative violations than its resources can address, the agency must regularly exercise prosecutorial discretion to prioritize its efforts. The memorandum provides a list of criteria for ICE personnel to use when assessing whether an individual case is appropriate for an exercise of prosecutorial discretion. In a second memorandum, also issued in June 2011, ICE provided additional guidance on the use of prosecutorial discretion for victims, witnesses, and plaintiffs.[21] Specifically, the additional guidance stated that ICE is to exercise discretion on a case-by-case basis when making detention and enforcement decisions in the cases of (1) victims of domestic violence, human trafficking, or other serious crimes; (2) witnesses involved in pending criminal investigations, plaintiffs in nonfrivolous lawsuits regarding civil rights or civil liberties violations; and (3) individuals engaging in a protected activity related to civil or other rights, such as union organizing.[22] In August 2011, DHS began to review all incoming cases in immigration court to identify the cases most clearly eligible and ineligible for exercising discretion to not pursue removal of the individual. DHS and DOJ launched pilot programs in which an intra-agency team of attorneys from ICE, U.S. Citizenship and Immigration Services, and U.S. Customs and Border Protection applied the June 2011 memorandums to its review of existing cases in the

---

[20]ICE, *Exercising Prosecutorial Discretion Consistent with the Civil Immigration Enforcement Priorities of the Agency for the Apprehension, Detention, and Removal of Aliens* (Washington, D.C.: June 17, 2011). Prosecutorial discretion is the authority of an agency charged with enforcing a law to decide to what degree to enforce the law against a particular individual.

[21]ICE, *Prosecutorial Discretion: Certain Victims, Witnesses, and Plaintiffs* (Washington, D.C.: June 17, 2011).

[22]In 2007, GAO recommended that ICE consider analyzing trends in the use of prosecutorial discretion, but ICE determined that it was not feasible given the multiple points throughout the immigration enforcement process where discretion could be applied. ICE issued the aforementioned prosecutorial discretion guidance in June 2011 to better reflect ICE civil immigration enforcement priorities and ensure consistency throughout the field in its use and implementation. GAO, *Immigration Enforcement: ICE Could Improve Controls to Help Guide Alien Removal Decision Making*, GAO 08-67 (Washington, D.C.: Oct. 15, 2007).

Denver and Baltimore immigration courts.[23] On March 30, 2012, DHS announced that in the next phase of its pilot, beginning in April 2012, it would extend its case reviews to immigration courts in Seattle, Detroit, New Orleans, Orlando, New York City, San Francisco, and Los Angeles.

ICE has followed an incremental approach to activating Secure Communities interoperability in jurisdictions nationwide.[24] Since August 2011, ICE has been simultaneously activating all jurisdictions within a given state into Secure Communities. From October 2008 to August 2011, ICE activated 1,508 jurisdictions after signing individual memorandums of agreement with their respective state governments. In August 2011, ICE terminated all existing memorandums of agreement, stating that they were not required because once a law enforcement agency voluntarily submits fingerprint data to the federal government, no agreement with the state is legally necessary for one part of the federal government to share it with another part.

As of June 5, 2012, ICE had fully activated Secure Communities in all jurisdictions in 48 states, the District of Columbia, and four United States territories.[25] Additionally, the program has been partially activated in 2 states. The 50 states where Secure Communities has been fully or partially activated cover 97 percent of jurisdictions nationwide. ICE plans to have all jurisdictions in all 50 states and U.S. territories activated by March 2013. Figure 2 depicts the states activated under Secure Communities as of June 5, 2012.

---

[23]The ICE Principal Legal Advisor issued a memorandum to all Offices of Chief Counsel in the field providing guidance on these efforts. ICE, Office of the Principal Legal Advisor, *Case-by-Case Review of Incoming and Certain Pending Cases* (Washington, D.C.: Nov. 17, 2011).

[24]A jurisdiction is activated when interoperability between IAFIS and IDENT becomes functional for that location. For purposes of this report, jurisdiction is synonymous with county or a county-equivalent.

[25]The four U.S. territories where Secure Communities is fully activated are American Samoa, Guam, Puerto Rico, and the U.S. Virgin Islands. ICE has not yet activated Secure Communities in the Commonwealth of the Northern Mariana Islands.

Figure 2: Secure Communities Activation Status as of June 5, 2012

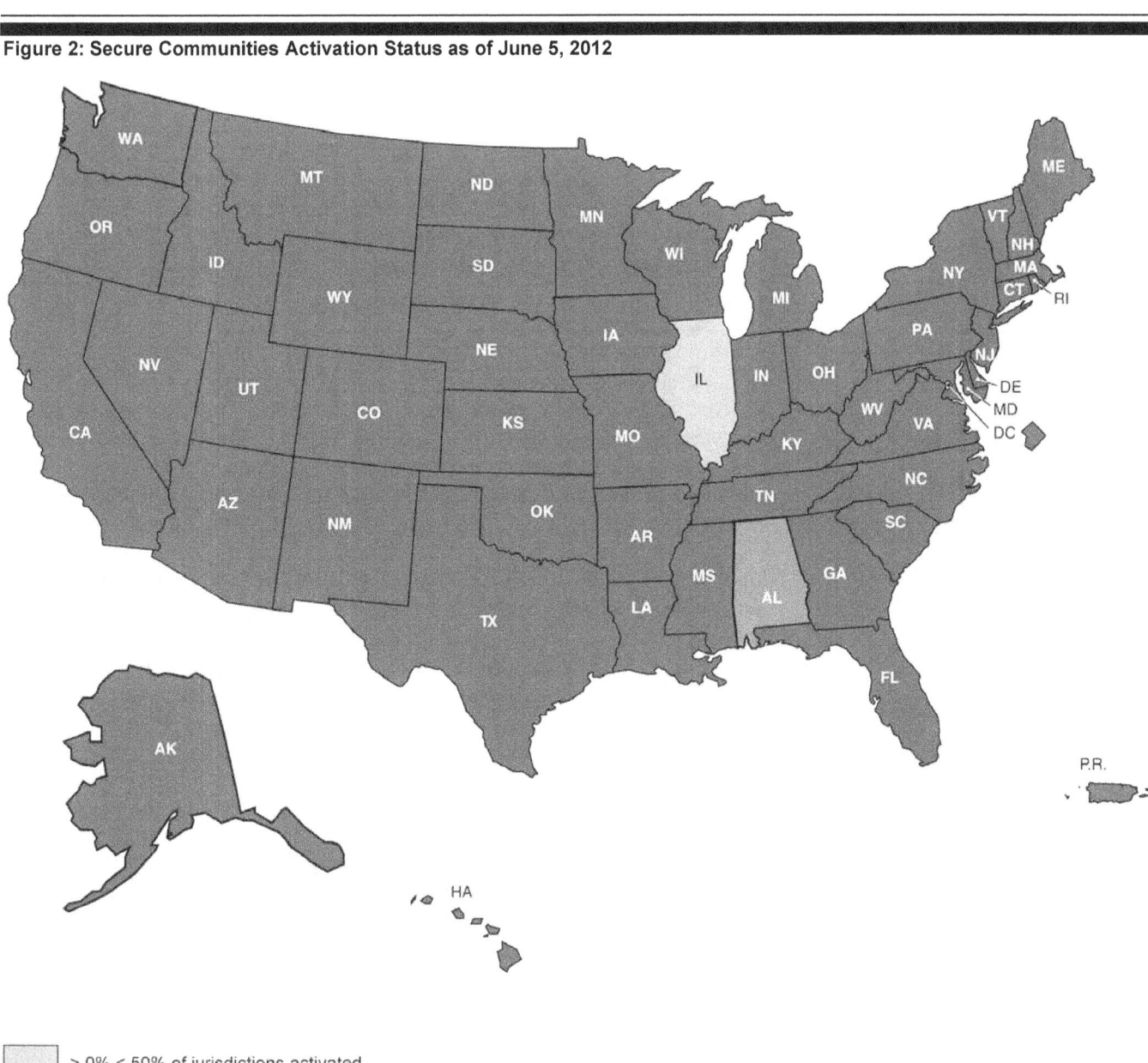

> 0% < 50% of jurisdictions activated

≥ 50% < 100% of jurisdictions activated

100% of jurisdictions activated

Source: GAO anaylsis of data provided by ICE.

DHS's CRCL is statutorily responsible for assisting DHS components in ensuring that the protection of civil rights and civil liberties is appropriately incorporated into DHS activities and programs, including Secure Communities.[26] CRCL is responsible, among other things, for investigating public complaints about DHS to ensure that DHS's policies promote respect for civil rights and civil liberties both within DHS and in conjunction with state and local partners. Investigating and resolving civil rights and civil liberties complaints filed by the public, including claims of racial profiling, is an area of focus for CRCL.[27]

Most Secure Communities Removals Were Criminal Aliens, but Arrest Charge Data Are Incomplete

ICE data show that from October 2008 through March 2012, Secure Communities led to the removal of about 183,000 aliens, of which approximately 74 percent had a criminal conviction and 26 percent did not have a criminal conviction known to ICE. All four ICE field offices we visited were using agency policies to help determine which aliens identified by Secure Communities should be selected for detention and removal. Additionally, ICE did not have a record of the state or local arrest charges for about 56 percent of the aliens that Secure Communities identified and ICE removed during fiscal year 2011 and the first half of fiscal year 2012, so we were unable to determine the most frequent arrest charges of aliens removed under the program. Of the data that ICE collected, traffic offenses were the most frequent arrest charges, of which over half were arrests for driving under the influence of alcohol.

Secure Communities Removals Have Increased, and ICE Data Show That the Majority of Aliens Removed Had Criminal Convictions

ICE data indicate that the percentage of removals attributable to Secure Communities has increased from fiscal year 2009 through the first 6 months of fiscal year 2012 and that nearly three-fourths of aliens removed under the program during this time frame had a criminal conviction. As shown in table 2, Secure Communities was responsible for identifying about 20 percent of the approximately 400,000 aliens that ICE removed in fiscal year 2011, up from approximately 4 percent of the aliens that ICE removed in fiscal year 2009. Other ICE enforcement programs such as CAP and 287(g) were responsible for identifying the majority of aliens that ICE removed in each year since fiscal year 2009.

---

[26]6 U.S.C. § 345(a)(3).

[27]6 U.S.C. § 345(a)(1), (4), (6).

Table 2: Number and Percentage of ICE's Removals Attributed to Secure Communities, by Fiscal Year

Year	ICE removals	Removals attributed to Secure Communities	Percentage of ICE removals attributed to Secure Communities
2009	389,834	14,363	4%
2010	392,862	49,498	13%
2011	396,606	79,876	20%
2012: October 2011 through March 2012	187,763	39,159	21%
Total	**1,367,065**	**182,896**	**13%**

Source: GAO analysis of data provided by ICE.

From October 2008 through March 2012, ICE removed 182,896 aliens identified by Secure Communities, as indicated by ICE's data. According to ICE, all aliens removed committed an immigration violation and were removable on that basis. About 74 percent had been convicted of a criminal offense; that is, they were either convicted of the offense that led to their identification under Secure Communities or had a record of conviction for a previous offense.[28] For these individuals, the current or prior criminal conviction served as the basis for ICE's prioritization for removal. Twenty-one percent of aliens removed did not have a criminal conviction known to ICE prior to their removal, but were identified as one of ICE's other removal priorities, including aliens who were fugitives or who reentered the country illegally after removal.[29] The remaining 5 percent of aliens removed also did not have a known criminal conviction prior to their removal but were nonetheless removable because, for example, they entered the United States without inspection or violated the terms of their admission. ICE reports its removal data for aliens without a criminal conviction under three categories: ICE fugitives; prior removals and returns; and entries without inspection (EWI) and visa violators. Figure 3 provides information on the overall composition of Secure

---

[28]In making removal determinations, ICE does not consider the period of time that has elapsed since the alien's previous criminal conviction(s), according to an Assistant Director in ERO.

[29]ICE officials indicated that there are several reasons why aliens identified by Secure Communities and removed may not have had a criminal conviction known to ICE at the time ICE took custody. For example, the aliens may not have been convicted of the current criminal charge(s) for which they were arrested; their criminal charge(s) were pending; or their criminal conviction(s) records were not available to ICE.

Communities removals by category and figure 4 provides this information for each activated state.

Figure 3: Classification of 182,896 Aliens Who Were Removed by ICE after Being Identified by Secure Communities from October 2008 through March 2012

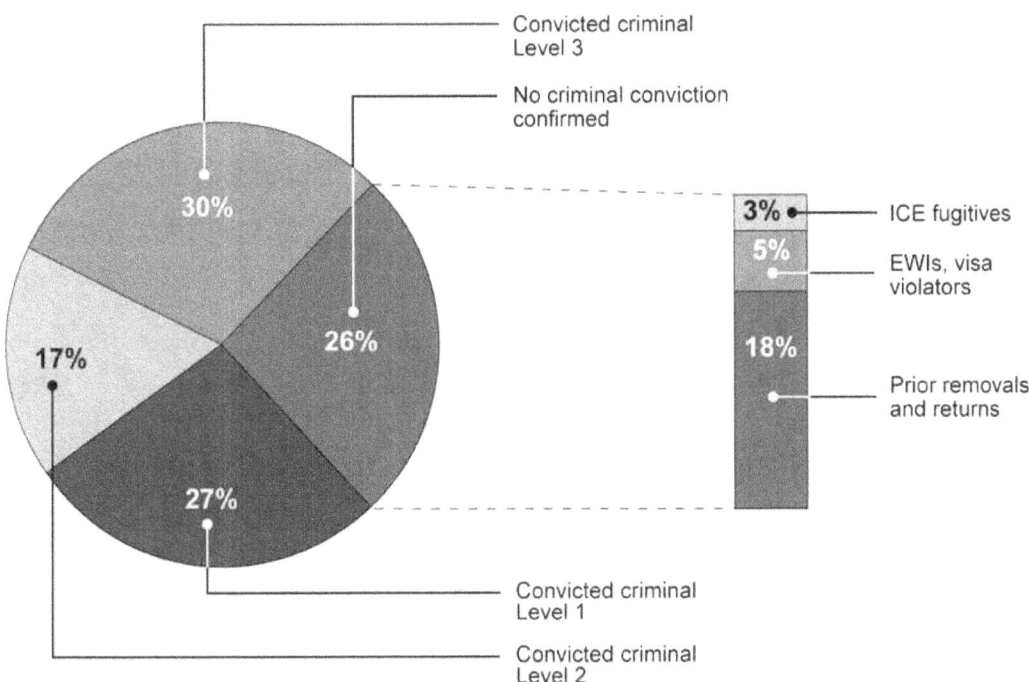

Category	Definition Category
Convicted criminal level 1	Includes aliens convicted of "aggravated felonies," as defined in § 101(a)(43) of the Immigration and Nationality Act, or two or more crimes punishable by more than one year, commonly referred to as "felonies."
Convicted criminal level 2	Includes aliens convicted of any felony or three or more offenses punishable by less than one year, commonly referred to as "misdemeanors."
Convicted criminal level 3	Includes aliens convicted of offenses punishable by less than one year.
ICE fugitives	Includes aliens who do not have a recorded criminal conviction confirmed by ICE, but have failed to leave the United States following the issuance of a final order of removal, deportation, or exclusion.
Prior removals and returns	Includes aliens who do not have a recorded criminal conviction confirmed by ICE, are not classified as ICE fugitives, but have had a previous removal case or confirmed return entered in DHS systems.
Entries without inspection (EWI), visa violators	Includes aliens who do not have a recorded criminal conviction confirmed by ICE and are not classified as ICE fugitives or prior removals or returns. Examples include aliens who entered the United States without inspection or violated the terms of their admission.

Source: GAO analysis of information provided by ICE.

Note: ICE fugitives, EWIs, visa violators, and prior removals and returns are not mutually exclusive categories. Therefore, for the approximately 26 percent of aliens removed without a confirmed criminal conviction, ICE reported that it will use the highest priority category for reporting purposes. For example, an alien who enters the United States without inspection (EWI) who is also an ICE fugitive would be reported as an ICE fugitive.

Figure 4: Arrest locations of Aliens Identified by Secure Communities and Removed by ICE, From October 2008 through March 2012

Move mouse over the name of each state to view the percentage of aliens arrested in the state removed from the United States who were classified in each category.

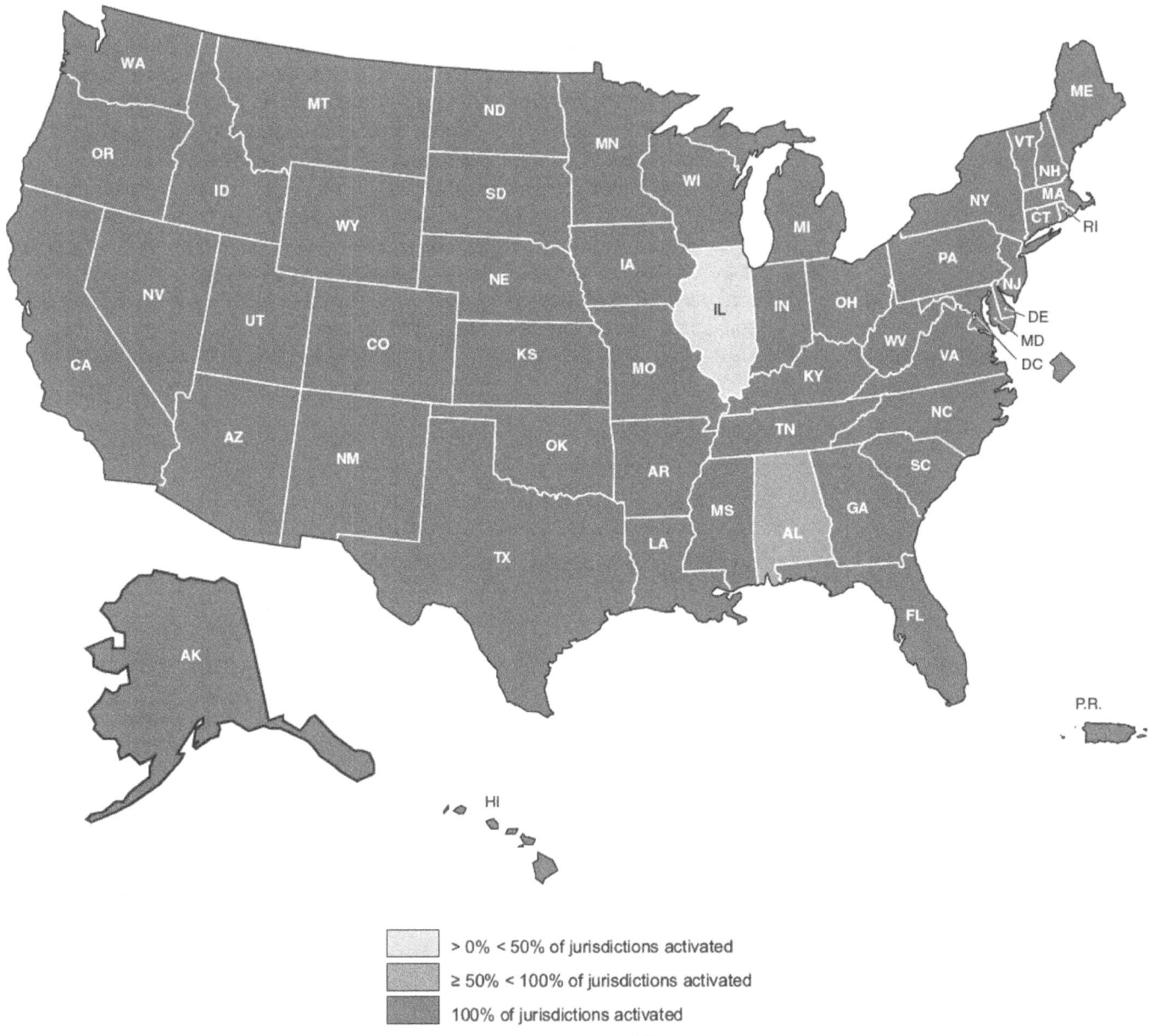

> 0% < 50% of jurisdictions activated

≥ 50% < 100% of jurisdictions activated

100% of jurisdictions activated

Source: GAO anaylsis of data provided by ICE.

Note: The number of Secure Communities removals for each state reflects, in part, the period of time he state has been ac ivated under the program.

Percentages may not add to 100 due to rounding.

ICE reported that the total number of Secure Communities removals has increased each year since fiscal year 2009, but there has been some variation across fiscal years in the proportion of aliens removed by criminal level, as shown in figure 5. For example, there was a decrease in the proportion of convicted criminal Level 3 offenders removed, from 40 percent of total removals in fiscal year 2009 to 26 percent during the first half of fiscal year 2012. According to ICE, the percentage of removals who are Level 3 offenders has been decreasing, in part because ICE has continued to prioritize its resources on the identification and removal of aliens convicted of felonies. Additionally, ICE redefined its criminal offense levels between fiscal years 2010 and 2011, causing some Level 3 offenders to be reclassified as Level 2 offenders based upon repeat misdemeanor offenses, which ICE officials said resulted in an increase in the percentage of removals who were Level 2 offenders to 19 percent in fiscal year 2011 as compared with 13 percent in fiscal year 2010, and a decrease in the percentage classified as level 3.

Figure 5: Composition of Secure Communities Removals by Fiscal Year

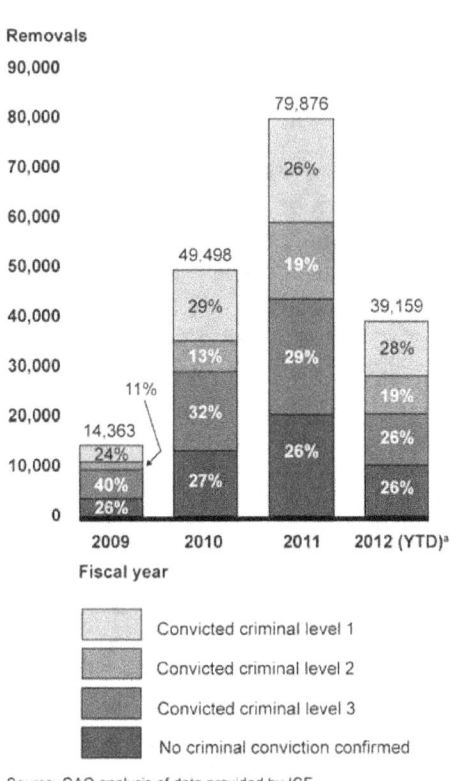

Source: GAO analysis of data provided by ICE

[a]For fiscal year 2012 year to date (YTD), data is through March 31, 2012.

Note: Percentages may not add to 100 due to rounding.

ICE's removal data do not reflect those aliens identified as removable through the Secure Communities program who are currently serving criminal sentences in state and local prisons, as ICE has not yet detained and removed them. For example, an alien arrested and identified through Secure Communities who is then convicted of a felony and classified by ICE as convicted criminal Level 1 offender is more likely to serve a longer criminal sentence than a Level 3 offender serving a sentence of less than 1 year. As a result, according to ICE, the percentage of Secure Communities removals who are Level 1 offenders—ICE's highest removal priority—could increase over time as Level 1 offenders complete their sentences and are removed.

Officials from the four ICE field offices we visited told us that they were following agency policies to help determine which aliens identified by

Secure Communities should be selected for detention and removal, and establishing the criminal offense level for each alien. ICE officials said that aliens are initially classified as Level 1, 2, or 3, based on the offense category definitions explained in the March 2011 priorities memorandum, and available information on the aliens' arrest charges and any previous convictions. ICE staff told us that they then use this offense level classification to prioritize which aliens should be detained.[30] ICE officials said that investigative actions are first focused on aliens who are initially classified as Level 1, but those classified as Level 2 and 3 may also be investigated if field offices have the resources to do so. At all four field offices we visited, ICE officials said that they generally have the resources to investigate the immigration and criminal histories of aliens initially classified as Level 1 and Level 2. Officials at three of the field offices said they also investigate aliens initially classified as Level 3, but do so only when the office has no one in the Level 1 or 2 category awaiting review. At the fourth field office, officials said that with their current resources, they can investigate all aliens initially classified as Level 1, 2, and 3.

ICE Had Incomplete Data on Arrest Charges for Over Half of the Aliens It Removed under Secure Communities

ICE did not have a record of the state or local arrest charges for about 56 percent of the approximately 119,000 aliens that Secure Communities identified and ICE removed during fiscal year 2011 and the first half of fiscal year 2012, so we were unable to determine the most frequent arrest charges of aliens removed under the program. ICE officials said that their records are incomplete because arrest charge information is not always available at the time ICE agents record aliens' criminal encounters and because agents may not have been familiar with a requirement, instituted by ICE in October 2010, to enter this information into ICE's database of investigations, arrests, bookings, detention, and removals. ICE issued guidance in August 2010 in advance of this requirement, and began offering training to its agents in the field on the agency's process for entering criminal arrest charge information into ICE's database. Further, ICE instituted a measure in November 2011 that calls for its data analysis unit to check on a monthly basis the criminal history database entries of aliens who did not have convictions at the time of their removal. If the check returns updated conviction data for these aliens, according to its

---

[30]This initial classification may be different from the classification of an alien upon removal if ICE obtains additional information before the alien is removed. For example, ICE could change the classification if the alien's charges are dropped or if previous convictions are identified.

guidance, ICE is to update its database to ensure that all available arrest and conviction data are included. ICE officials told us in May 2012 that going forward they expect to have arrest and conviction history data on a higher percentage of aliens as a result of these steps. As these efforts have only recently been initiated, it is too early to assess the effectiveness of ICE's efforts to improve the collection of arrest charge data.

Of the data ICE did collect, about 37 percent of aliens identified by Secure Communities and removed during fiscal year 2011 and the first half of fiscal year 2012 were arrested for traffic offenses (of whom over half were charged with driving while under the influence of alcohol), about 12 percent were arrested for drug offenses (of whom almost one-third were charged with marijuana offenses), about 10 percent were arrested for assault (of whom over half were arrested for unspecified assaults), and the remaining 40 percent were arrested for other offenses. Table 3 provides the available arrest charge information of aliens that Secure Communities identified and ICE removed during fiscal year 2011 and the first half of fiscal year 2012.

Table 3: Arrest Charge Information for Aliens That Secure Communities Identified and ICE Removed during Fiscal Year 2011 and the First Half of Fiscal Year 2012, Including the Most Frequent Arrest Charge Categories

	Aliens that Secure Communities identified and ICE removed	
	Number	**Percent**
Arrest charge information not available	66,855	56
Arrest charge information available	52,180	44
Total	**119,035**	**100**
Most frequent arrest charge categories of aliens on whom ICE had arrest charge information		
Traffic offenses[a]	19,526	37
Dangerous drugs[b]	6,489	12
Assault[c]	5,185	10
Other[d]	20,980	40
Total	**52,180**	**100**

Source: GAO analysis of data provided by ICE.

Note: Percentages may not add to 100 because of rounding.

[a]According to ICE's data, the traffic offenses category includes the following crimes: driving under the influence of alcohol or drugs, hit and run, transporting dangerous material, and other unspecified traffic offenses.

[b]The dangerous drugs category includes arrests for amphetamines, barbiturates, cocaine, hallucinogens, heroin, marijuana, opium, synthetic narcotics, and other unspecified drug offenses.

[c]The assault category includes the following crimes: unspecified assault, battery, domestic violence, intimidation, simple assault, and various aggravated assaults.

[d]Other arrest charge categories include, for example, larceny; burglary; fraudulent activities; obstructing the police; forgery; weapon offenses; vehicle theft; sexual assault; robbery; kidnapping; homicide; smuggling; arson; embezzlement; and extortion.

ICE Is Modernizing Its Technology System for Determining Immigration Status, but Acquisition and Implementation Planning Could Be Improved

ICE is modernizing its ACRIMe system to make the process of determining an individual's immigration status more efficient, but these efforts have experienced delays and cost overruns, and developed products that did not meet mission needs. ICE could mitigate the risk of further delays and cost overruns by better defining the ACRIMe program's requirements and developing an integrated master schedule. ICE could also better plan its future workforce needs to help realize the anticipated efficiency gains of the modernized ACRIMe system.

ICE Is Modernizing Its ACRIMe System

ICE is in the process of developing a modernized ACRIMe system to update its aging legacy system and meet the anticipated increase in the number of law enforcement queries as Secure Communities is implemented in more jurisdictions across the country. The modernized ACRIMe system is designed to be accessible throughout ICE and not just in LESC, as is currently the case. Additionally, to help determine an individual's immigration status and offense category, modernized ACRIMe is intended to allow officials in LESC, ICE field offices, and response centers to automatically search multiple data sources with a single electronic query. Currently, LESC staff must conduct separate searches to obtain information from separate databases and, because of limitations in the legacy ACRIMe system, they cannot share the full results of their searches with staff in ICE field offices and response centers. Since the modernized ACRIMe system is intended to allow users to search, receive, distribute, and manage relevant immigration status information, ICE officials expect that the modernized system will eliminate the need for ICE field office and response center staff to duplicate LESC's efforts to determine aliens' immigration status.

ICE initially planned to develop the modernized ACRIMe system through three contracts, each for a separate project. The first contract (referred to here as ACRIMe-1), awarded in March 2008, was to develop a modernized ACRIMe system so ICE staff could access multiple law enforcement and immigration databases to determine an individual's immigration status and offense category.[31] ICE awarded two additional contracts in September 2009 to develop six services to further enhance the functionality of the modernized ACRIMe system. One contract was to develop a web-based Automated Threat Prioritization (ATP) service that would allow modernized ACRIMe users to automatically retrieve prior conviction information from state and federal criminal history records to help prioritize ICE enforcement actions based on aliens' criminal charges. The other contract, the Status Determination Support (SDS) contract, was to develop five web-based services to enhance the modernized ACRIMe system's ability to determine immigration status. The five services were (1) Status Determination Support, (2) Automated National Crime Information Center Warrants, (3) Criminal Alien Tracking, (4) Jail Roster/Release Tracking, and (5) Integrated Case Management.[32] Table 4 provides summary information on the three ACRIMe modernization projects and the contracts issued in 2008 and 2009.

---

[31]The contract that ICE awarded in 2008 to acquire the modernized ACRIMe system was also to acquire other technology-related services. We use the term "ACRIMe-1" to refer to the portion of the contract related to acquiring the modernized ACRIMe system.

[32]The Status Determination Support service (a subcomponent of the overall SDS contract) provides an automated search of multiple disparate databases and creates a most likely immigration status determination for verification by ICE officials. The Automated National Crime Information Center Warrants service automates the process for entering new warrants and searching, updating and revalidating existing warrants. Criminal Alien Tracking is a web service to automate the tracking of aliens to allow ICE to begin removal proceedings while aliens are in criminal custody. Jail Roster/Release Tracking is a web service to provide ICE the ability to receive rosters of jail inmates so it could determine the time frame for a criminal alien's removability. The Integrated Case Management service automates the collection of criminal alien status information in designated case management systems.

Table 4: ACRIMe Modernization Projects

Dollars in millions

Project	Project baseline cost estimate[a]	Contract	Date contract awarded
Modernized ACRIMe System: To develop a modernized ACRIMe system for accessing multiple law enforcement and immigration databases	$10.3	ACRIMe-1	March 2008
ATP Service: To develop a web-based service to allow modernized ACRIMe users to automatically retrieve prior conviction information from state and federal criminal history records.	18.3	ATP	September 2009
SDS Services: To develop web services to enhance modernized ACRIMe's capability to determine immigration status: • Status Determination Support • Automated National Crime Information Center Warrants • Criminal Alien Tracking • Jail Roster/Release Tracking • Integrated Case Management	41.7	SDS	September 2009

Source: GAO analysis of ICE information.

[a]The project baseline cost estimate for the Modernized ACRIMe System was an independent government cost estimate developed by ICE. The project baseline cost estimates for the ATP and SDS services were acquisition cost estimates that ICE issued in its July 2009 *Criminal Alien Identification Initiative Acquisition Program Baseline* plan.

Weaknesses in ICE's ACRIMe Modernization Planning Contributed to Delays, Cost Increases, and Products That Did Not Meet Mission Needs

Weaknesses in ICE's acquisition planning contributed to delays, cost increases, and products provided under the contracts that did not meet mission needs. As of April 2012, ICE had spent approximately $4 million over its original cost estimate to develop the modernized ACRIMe system—without the ATP and SDS services—and expected that it would begin deploying the system in LESC in July 2012 and in ICE field offices in December 2012. This date is over 2 years after the initial planned deployment date of March 2010 for the ACRIMe system. Further, the contractor that ICE selected for the ACRIMe-1 contract did not develop a system that met ICE's performance requirements. As a result, ICE canceled the ACRIMe-1 contract, selected a new contractor in September 2011 to complete and deploy the modernized system, and expects to award another contract by September 2012 to develop call center functionalities within the modernized ACRIMe system that were originally supposed to be delivered through the ACRIMe-1 contract. In August 2011, ICE also canceled the original SDS contract because of the delays encountered with the ACRIMe-1 contract. Further, because of its dissatisfaction with the quality of the work completed on the SDS contract, ICE now plans to award additional contracts to different contractors to start over with developing the services it requires. ICE has also reduced the scope of the SDS services' capabilities (as discussed below). As a result, ICE expects that the SDS services will be completed for about $22 million less than the baseline cost estimate, even though it spent $14.3 million on a contract that did not produce useable services. In contrast, ICE has expanded the scope of the ATP requirements and expects to exceed its baseline cost estimate by about $7.8 million. ICE projects that for the ATP and SDS services, it will be able to meet and potentially finish ahead of its estimated deployment dates. See appendix I for additional information on all of ICE's ACRIMe-related contracts. Table 5 compares the baseline estimates for deployment and cost of the projects, and status as of April 2012.

Table 5: Comparison of Schedule and Cost Estimates

Dollars in millions

	Scheduled deployment date[a]		Project costs[b]	
Project	Baseline	As of April 2012	Baseline	Estimate as of April 2012
Modernized ACRIMe System[c]	March 2010	July 2012	$10.3	$21.8
ATP Service	December 2013	December 2012	18.3	26.1
SDS Services[d]	December 2013	June 2013	41.7	19.7

Source: GAO analysis of ICE information.

[a]The deployment dates are the dates for the initial operational capability, rather than the final operational capability. ICE is using an iterative approach, and officials expect that some additional work will be needed after the initial deployment before the technology is fully functional. ICE officials told us they expect the three projects to be fully operational by March 2014.

[b]The project baseline cost estimate for the modernized ACRIMe system was an independent government cost estimate developed by ICE. The project baseline cost estimates for the ATP and SDS services were acquisition cost estimates that ICE issued in its July 2009 *Criminal Alien Identification Initiative Acquisition Program Baseline* plan. The project cost estimates as of April 2012 for the modernized ACRIMe System and the SDS services were calculated by adding the total amount ICE has funded on the canceled contracts (the ACRIME-1 and SDS contracts, respectively) to the estimated value of the contracts ICE has awarded or plans to award to complete the projects. For the ATP service, the estimated project cost is the value of the contract listed in the most recent contract modification as of April 2012.

[c]The original contract was terminated and a new contractor hired for the work. The second contract is to complete and deploy the system as well as to provide ongoing operations and maintenance through August 2016. As of April 2012, ICE had spent $14.4 million on acquiring the modernized ACRIMe system under both contracts. ICE also plans to award another contract by September 2012, to develop call center functionalities within the modernized ACRIMe system.

[d]The original SDS contract was canceled without the services being delivered. ICE plans to award new contracts to develop the services.

The schedule delays and cost increases can be attributed in part to weaknesses in ICE's planning, including ICE (1) not fully defining requirements before awarding contracts and (2) not developing an integrated master schedule.

Defining Requirements

According to ICE officials, the agency did not fully define its requirements before awarding the ACRIMe-1, ATP, or SDS contracts. We have previously reported that firm requirements should be established at the beginning of an acquisition program and that requirements should be well defined to ensure communication about what the government needs from the contractor providing services.[33]

Regarding the ACRIMe-1 contract, ICE officials stated that ICE's requirements did not accurately reflect the needs of LESC system users or fully define technical expectations. Although ICE involved LESC users in the development of the system requirements, ICE officials told us that ICE did not ensure the users' needs were clearly defined in the requirements documentation and the contractor did not routinely meet with the users to ensure its understanding of the requirements. As a result, the contractor misinterpreted some of the requirements, according to ICE officials. ICE revised the requirements after the contractor had already conducted a significant amount of work, contributing to delays. Further, ICE officials told us that ICE did not fully define its technical expectations of the contractor, such as specific requirements for the software code. According to the officials, ICE did not include more specific technical requirements because it wanted to encourage the contractor to develop innovative solutions and did not want to be too prescriptive. However, the officials also noted that not having more specific technical requirements contributed to the unsatisfactory performance by the contractor in producing software that did not meet ICE's needs. Consequently, ICE deemed the modernized ACRIMe system the contractor delivered in April 2011 to be unusable, and ICE awarded a new contract in September 2011 to a different contractor to complete and deploy the system. ICE also plans to award another contract for $1.7 million by September 2012, to develop call center functionalities within the ACRIMe system that were originally supposed to be developed under the ACRIMe-1 contract.

---

[33]See GAO, *Immigration Benefits: Consistent Adherence to DHS's Acquisition Policy Could Help Improve Transformation Program*, GAO-12-66 (Washington, D.C.: Nov. 22, 2011), and GAO-08-619.

Shortcomings in defining requirements and changes in the scope of the requirements also contributed to cost increases on the ATP contract. Specifically, cost increases occurred when, in August 2011, nearly 2 years after the ATP contract was awarded, ICE added a new requirement that the contractor develop a "risk classification assessment score." This score is meant to help standardize the method for determining if an alien should be detained by ICE or released on bond or other condition. According to ICE, the requirement for a risk classification assessment score was added to the ATP contract to support ICE detention reform initiatives based on revisions that were made in 2011 to ICE's detention standards. Among other things, the 2011 detention standards call for detention facilities to take into account risk factors when making custody decisions.[34] Officials told us it would be more efficient to add the risk classification assessment score requirement to the ATP contract than to develop this capability through a separate system. However, the officials also stated that ICE could do a better job of defining its requirements. As of April 2011, ICE had spent about $21.5 million on acquiring the ATP service, which is about 17 percent over ICE's baseline cost estimate of $18.3 million. To complete the ATP service, ICE estimates that it may need to spend an additional $4.6 million, for a total cost of $26.1 million. This would be a 42 percent increase over ICE's baseline cost estimate.

With respect to the SDS contract, in September 2010, about a year after the SDS contract was awarded (and over 2 years after ACRIMe-1 was awarded), ICE determined that the SDS contract requirements overlapped significantly with those of the ACRIMe-1 contract. In response, ICE expanded the scope of the SDS contract to include all of the requirements for aggregating data from multiple law enforcement and immigration databases that had previously been spread between the ACRIMe-1 and SDS contracts, and eliminated the requirements from the ACRIMe-1 contract. ICE officials stated that not clearly defining how the SDS services would be integrated with the ACRIMe system was an oversight. As with the ACRIMe-1 contract, ICE officials stated that the technical requirements for the contract were not well defined, and this contributed to the contractor producing poor-quality software. Consequently, ICE spent $14.3 million for the SDS contract to develop services that ICE found to be unusable. ICE terminated the SDS contract in August 2011. As of April 2012, ICE officials planned to award four new

---

[34]ICE, *Performance-Based National Detention Standards 2011*.

contracts at an estimated total cost of $5.4 million that would involve the contractors starting over with developing services to enhance the functionality of the modernized ACRIMe system. In commenting on a draft of this report, in June 2012 ICE officials told us that to complete the SDS services, they now plan to award two (instead of four) new contracts and that they are incorporating the work that would have been done through the two other previously planned contracts into other ACRIMe modernization efforts.[35]

According to ICE officials, some of the documents the SDS contractor developed, such as the Concept of Operations, will be used to help inform future contractors' work. ICE officials noted that despite spending $14.3 million on the SDS contract, which did not produce useable functionalities, ICE expects to spend about $22 million less than the original cost estimate of $41.7 million because the scope of capabilities to be provided by the contractor have been reduced. Specifically, ICE found after awarding the SDS contract that it would be more technically complicated and costly to develop the criminal alien tracking service than it had anticipated, so ICE does not plan to pursue the development of this functionality further. ICE officials acknowledged the importance of establishing well-defined requirements going forward, but as of April 2012, ICE had not developed the requirements for the contracts it planned to award starting in July 2012 through December 2012.[36] In light of the challenges it has experienced as a result of unclear and changing requirements, ICE could be better positioned to help prevent delays and cost increases by establishing well-defined requirements that accurately reflect both user and technical needs prior to awarding additional contracts.

Developing an Integrated Master Schedule

Although ICE anticipates meeting its baseline deployment dates for the SDS services that it plans to develop through new contracts, it has not developed an integrated master schedule for completing ACRIMe modernization. Rather, ICE has used the separate schedules developed for each contract to manage the modernization effort. We have previously reported that one critical management tool for complex systems that

---

[35] The contracts to be awarded are for four of the five services initially to be delivered under the SDS contract. We will continue to monitor these efforts as part of our recommendation follow-up work. See appendix I for additional information.

[36] See appendix I for additional information on the ACRIMe modernization contracts.

involve the incorporation of a number of different projects—in this case, ACRIMe modernization—is an integrated master schedule that allows managers to monitor all work activities, how long the activities will take, and how the activities are related to one another.[37] Because ICE lacked an integrated master schedule when it issued the first three ACRIMe modernization contracts in 2008 and 2009, it was not well positioned to understand how schedule changes in each individual contract would affect the overall modernization effort. For example, ICE assumed that the modernized ACRIMe system would be completed before work began on the ATP and SDS contracts. However, the deployment of the modernized ACRIMe system was delayed, and because ICE did not have an integrated master schedule, ICE was not in a position to effectively identify and resolve the effects of delays in the deployment of the modernized ACRIMe system on the development of the SDS and ATP services. Subsequently, the delays with the deployment of the modernized ACRIMe system contributed to the cancellation of the SDS contract and delayed the integration of the ATP service with the modernized ACRIMe system, according to ICE officials.

Even though ICE delayed deployment of the modernized ACRIMe system and canceled the original SDS contract, it projects that the ATP service will be deployed in December 2012, and the SDS services will be deployed by the end of June 2013, both ahead of ICE's baseline initial deployment estimate of December 2013. ICE officials explained that the initial deployment dates were based on outdated information and that ICE has since reduced the scope of the requirements needed for the SDS services because it now has a better understanding of those requirements. Further, ICE officials said they have learned to work with contractors more effectively to produce results in a timely manner by using an incremental development approach.[38] ICE developed a deployment schedule for ACRIMe and its SDS and ATP services, but this schedule did not include elements of a reliable integrated master schedule, such as listings of all activities to be completed. ICE officials stated that their estimate of deployment for the SDS and ATP services

---

[37] GAO-09-3SP.

[38] ICE is using an incremental development approach called "Agile software development." Agile software development is a philosophy based on selected values, such as the highest priority is to satisfy customers through early and continuous delivery of valuable software; delivering working software frequently; and that working software is the primary measure of progress.

was based on their knowledge of the remaining work to be done and past experience developing schedules. However, they acknowledged that by not developing an integrated master schedule, ICE did not meet best practices for managing capital programs and recognized the importance of having an integrated master schedule moving forward. Accordingly, ICE officials said they began developing an integrated master schedule in April 2012, during the course of our review. While we recognize this as a positive step, it is too early to tell if ICE's efforts will result in an integrated master schedule that reflects all of the tasks to be completed by the agency and contractors. For example, as of May 2012, ICE had not incorporated detailed project schedules for the four SDS services into its integrated master schedule. GAO's *Cost Estimating and Assessment Guide* states that an integrated master schedule should include all tasks necessary to complete the project, including work to be performed by both the government and contractors.[39] Given the number of new contracts ICE plans to award and its previous difficulties with accounting for all contract activities and their interrelationships, ICE could help ensure that its deployment schedule is reliable and mitigate schedule risks by developing an integrated master schedule that includes all activities and identifies dependencies among the complementary contracts it plans to award.

Workforce Planning Could Improve Use of Resources under ACRIMe Modernization

Various developments could change ICE's workforce requirements for responding to state and local law enforcement's queries about aliens' immigration and criminal status, providing ICE with an opportunity to examine the most efficient number and location of staff to accomplish the task. One development is the anticipated deployment of modernized ACRIMe to ICE field offices in December 2012, which could help reduce the existing duplication of effort in analyzing immigration and criminal status information. This duplication of effort involves ICE field office staff repeating database searches that LESC has already conducted because ACRIMe, which LESC uses to determine individuals' immigration status, cannot generate reports or electronically transmit the results of LESC's

---

[39]We have previously identified other characteristics necessary to develop reliable schedules, but because ICE did not develop an integrated master schedule, we did not review the extent to which ICE conformed to other scheduling best practices. Other best practices include identifying resources, such as labor, material, and costs, needed for each activity, and conducting a schedule risk analysis, among others. For further discussion of characteristics of reliable schedules, see GAO-09-3SP, 218-224.

database searches to field offices; and field offices do not have access to ACRIMe, necessitating that they conduct their own database searches. According to ICE officials, such duplication of effort is necessary not only because of the current ACRIMe system's limitations, but also because it serves as a quality control to minimize the likelihood of ICE making an incorrect arrest or detention decision. Modernized ACRIMe is expected to reduce the total number of immigration status database searches because the system is intended to be able to generate a report on the databases searched and electronically transmit the results of those searches. Another development is the anticipated increase in Secure Communities matches as the program is activated nationwide. ICE estimates indicate that when Secure Communities interoperability is activated in all jurisdictions in fiscal year 2013, it expects an additional approximately 90,000 Secure Communities queries will be generated each year. In calendar year 2011, LESC conducted database searches based on about 423,550 Secure Communities matches.[40]

As of April 2012, ICE had not determined or planned for how many staff it will need to conduct these searches. The new system will be accessible not only to LESC, as is currently the case, but also to field offices and interoperability response centers (which were set up primarily to analyze an increased number of immigration status queries resulting from Secure Communities), making it possible for multiple organizational entities in ICE to conduct the database searches. LESC officials said that if they had 60 additional staff, LESC would be able to process all Secure Communities requests for database searches for the entire country when modernized ACRIMe is deployed; however, an expansion under way at the Los Angeles response center could also accommodate additional staff for processing Secure Communities database searches. ICE officials have not yet addressed the role that LESC, the field-based response centers, or other ICE components involved with immigration status determination will have after modernized ACRIMe becomes operational.

In its April 2012 report, DHS's Inspector General recommended that ICE develop procedures to eliminate duplication in the process of identifying potentially removable criminal aliens. Further, congressional staff requested that ICE brief members in March 2012 regarding the efficient

---

[40]This figure represents all biometric Immigration Alien Queries (IAQ) received in fiscal year 2011, which also includes U.S. citizen biometric IAQs.

allocation of resources between LESC and the response centers; however, the briefing had not been scheduled as of June 8, 2012. *Standards for Internal Control in the Federal Government* identifies effective management of an organization's workforce as essential to achieving results and maintaining internal control, and program management guidance states that successful execution of any program includes developing plans that include efficient use of workforce resources.[41]

ICE officials acknowledged the need for comprehensive workforce planning, but officials indicated to us and to DHS's Office of Inspector General that the agency plans to wait until after Secure Communities is activated nationwide and modernized ACRIMe becomes operational in fiscal year 2013 to make decisions about how to effectively realign resources. In August 2011 ICE completed an Operational Workforce Analysis, which projected the additional ERO workforce needed for detention and removal when Secure Communities is fully activated. A separate ICE analysis provided estimates of the workforce needs at LESC for analyzing an additional 90,000 queries. ICE's analyses, however, did not consider the impact of modernized ACRIMe on workforce requirements or how staff resources at response centers will be utilized for making status determinations. Agency officials also said that uncertainty about funding was a factor they would need to consider as part of their planning. While planning efforts can be subject to uncertainty about future funding, developing a workforce plan prior to full program and system deployment could help position ICE so it is ready to effectively align staff among components responding to law enforcement agency queries when the modernized ACRIMe system is deployed.

---

[41]See GAO/AIMD-00-21.3.1 and the Project Management Institute's *The Standard for Program Management* (Newton Square, PA © 2006).

ICE and CRCL Identified Safeguards to Help Address Potential Civil Rights Abuses under Secure Communities; Some Efforts Have Not Yet Been Fully Implemented

ICE and CRCL jointly identified four safeguards used to help protect aliens' civil rights under Secure Communities. These safeguards include providing detainees a revised detainer form with telephone numbers to call when they believe their civil rights have been violated or they are U.S. citizens or crime victims, developing training materials for state and local law enforcement and ICE officials on how to protect aliens' civil rights, initiating a process to statistically monitor arrests under Secure Communities to identify and investigate potential patterns of civil rights abuses, and using DHS's existing complaint process to investigate complaints about possible civil rights abuses related to Secure Communities.

ICE's Revised Detainer Includes Phone Numbers for Detainees to Report Potential Abuse

ICE began using a revised detainer form in December 2011, in part as a safeguard against potential abuse of detainees. Changes on the form include a request that law enforcement officials provide the detainee a copy of the form, and to notify ICE if the individual may be the victim of a crime.[42] The revised form also includes a Notice to Detainee section printed in six languages with telephone numbers for arrested individuals to call. Calls for one number go to the LESC for individuals who believe they are U.S. citizens or victims of a crime and have been inappropriately identified for removal. The other number goes to the Joint Intake Center for individuals who believe their civil rights have been violated.[43] The detainer form is not specific to detainees identified under Secure Communities; ICE requests all detainees be given a copy of their detainer, regardless of how the detainees were identified. The English version of the notice is reproduced in figure 6.

---

[42]Officials from CRCL and ICE ERO stated that ICE does not have the authority to require that police departments or jails give a copy of the detainer form to the arrested individuals.

[43]The Joint Intake Center is operated by both ICE and U.S. Customs and Border Protection (CBP) personnel, and is responsible for receiving, classifying, and routing all misconduct allegations involving ICE and CBP employees, including those pertaining to detainee treatment. A list of all complaints received by the Center is sent monthly to CRCL for review under the DHS's agency-wide complaint process.

Figure 6: Detainer Form Notice to Detainee

Notice to Detainee
The Department of Homeland Security (DHS) has placed an immigration detainer on you. An immigration detainer is a notice from DHS informing law enforcement agencies that DHS intends to assume custody of you after you otherwise would be released from custody. DHS has requested that the law enforcement agency which is currently detaining you maintain custody of you for a period not to exceed 48 hours (excluding Saturdays, Sundays, and holidays) beyond the time when you would have been released by the state or local law enforcement authorities based on your criminal charges or convictions. If DHS does not take you into custody during that additional 48 hour period, not counting weekends or holidays, you should contact your custodian (the law enforcement agency or other entity that is holding you now) to inquire about your release from state or local custody. If you have a complaint regarding this detainer or related to violations of civil rights or civil liberties connected to DHS activities, please contact the ICE Joint Intake Center at 1877- 2INTAKE (877-246-8253). If you believe you are a United States citizen or the victim of a crime, please advise DHS by calling the ICE Law Enforcement Support Center at (855) 448-6903.

Source: Abstract from DHS Form 1-247 (12/11).

ICE detention management division officials said that the detainer is not the only avenue for individuals to be informed of whom to contact if they believe their civil rights have been violated. For example, officials said that once in ICE custody, detainees are given a handbook with steps to follow if they believe they were sexually assaulted or abused, or if they want to report other misconduct. Further, officials indicated that each facility housing detainees in ICE custody displays informational posters in detainee common areas with information on how to contact the DHS Office of the Inspector General.[44]

According to ICE data, calls to the LESC telephone number on the detainer form have not primarily been from detainees, and the calls have not primarily been made to report that a detainee is a U.S. citizen or a victim of a crime. LESC specialists fielded about 4,500 calls from December 26, 2011, to April 17, 2012, primarily from detainee family members and attorneys, often inquiring about the location of the detainee.[45] LESC officials said that each call is recorded and a written log is created. Of the calls received, LESC data indicated that 97 percent of the calls were "other;" that is, primarily detainee location questions, hang-ups, or calls to provide information on persons the caller believed might

---

[44]Detainees may file external complaints directly with the Office of the Inspector General, either in writing or by phone using the DHS Office of the Inspector General (OIG) complaint hotline. OIG may investigate the complaint or refer it to CRCL or DHS components such as the ICE Office of Professional Responsibility (OPR) for review and possible action.

[45]For such inquiries, callers are to be referred to ICE's online Detainee Locator System (www.ice.gov/locator).

be in the country illegally. Seventy-one, or 2 percent, of the calls concerned claims that the detainee was a U. S. citizen. According to LESC, of those claims, 11 of the 71 detainers were removed after the immigration status claim was investigated by LESC.[46] Fourteen callers stated that they were a victim of or witness to a crime, and the information was forwarded to the relevant local ICE office.

Illustrative examples from the LESC message logs (with names removed) are transcribed below:

- "Caller wanted to report some information involving an individual who paid someone to marry them just to gain status in the [United States]." (*Caller was referred to DHS's TipLine.*)

- "Caller stated he wanted to know the status of his brother's detainer. He had called yesterday and claimed his brother was a USC [United States Citizen]. The [agent] on site contacted the agent that placed the detainer yesterday, stating he would take the detainer off. After [agent X and agent Y] looked into it today the system did not show the detainer was lifted. It was lifted yesterday and updated in the system today. I advised caller he would need to call the local ICE office for more [information] to be able to ask the status of the case."

- "Caller stated she was looking for a friend that was being detained. I advised her to visit ICE.gov and use the detainee locator along with calling her local ICE office."

---

[46]LESC could not verify U.S. citizenship for 60 of the 71 calls relating to a claim of U.S. citizenship, and LESC did not remove the detainers for these individuals. LESC officials said they routed all 71 claims to the ICE field office that lodged the detainer to complete processing and conduct further analysis of the claim.

CRCL and ICE Are Developing Secure Communities Awareness Briefings for State and Local Law Enforcement Agencies

CRCL and ICE are collaborating to develop a series of modules to educate LEAs on civil rights and civil liberties issues that may arise under Secure Communities, as well as to reintroduce the program and its purpose.[47] The modules include videos and related materials, such as memorandums, legal materials, and handouts, for use by law enforcement agencies and training instructors. As of May 1, 2012, CRCL had released three of the eight videos that it plans to develop. These three videos are available on ICE's website, and ICE plans to share them with the law enforcement community through conferences and direct mailing of dissemination materials, according to CRCL. The remaining videos are in production and are expected to be completed by the end of calendar year 2012.

The first completed video, an Introduction to *Secure Communities for LEAs*, provides an overview of the program, including the expectation that law enforcement will not base any enforcement actions on factors such as race or ethnicity. The second video, *How to Respond to an Immigration Detainer*, explains to law enforcement personnel their role in responding to the new detainer and sharing information found on the new detainer form with the arrestee. The third video, *Consular Notification: Your Role when Detaining Foreign Nationals*, reiterates the importance of notifying foreign consulates when detaining non-U.S. citizens, a preexisting obligation under the Vienna Convention on Consular Relations.[48] Other planned videos include the following:

- *Avoiding Racial Profiling;*

- *Explaining Secure Communities to Your Community;*

- *Witnesses, Refugees and Victims of Crime or Domestic Violence: Protecting Those in Need;*

- *Retaliation by Private Actors; and*

- *Speaking Their Language: Working with Non-English Speakers*

---

[47]ICE officials acknowledge that there were limitations in communications regarding the purpose of the program when it was introduced in 2008.

[48]Vienna Convention on Consular Relations, art. 36, Apr. 24, 1963, 21 U.S.T. 77.

In May 2012, DHS established a dissemination plan for the Secure Communities videos, noting that ICE and CRCL plan to distribute the Secure Communities videos and materials to state and local LEAs. CRCL envisions that these agencies will share the information with law enforcement officers during routinely held briefings or in other settings.[49] Beginning in June 2011, CRCL distributed the first video to 117 LEAs and 143 nongovernmental organizations during visits made to eight major cities and at major conferences, such as the National Sheriff's Association conference. ICE also plans to provide the videos and materials to law enforcement training agencies and instructors in each state and to make the videos available as downloadable files on the Internet.

Data Complexities a Challenge in Analyzing Potential Arrest Anomalies under Secure Communities

To help determine whether local law enforcement agencies may be making inappropriate or unlawful arrests that could lead to removal through Secure Communities, CRCL and ICE developed a monitoring process in which Secure Communities–related statistics are reviewed on a quarterly basis. The monitoring process is designed to take place in three phases. In the first phase, CRCL's plan calls for analyzing crime, arrest, and demographic data from activated jurisdictions to determine the extent to which foreign-born individuals are arrested at a rate that is proportional to their representation in the jurisdiction's population, and the extent to which the types of charges for which foreign-born individuals are arrested are proportional to the types of arrest charges for all individuals in that jurisdiction.[50]

In the second phase, CRCL is conducting additional in-depth analyses of arrest, crime, and demographic data on the 10 large jurisdictions (those with populations over 100,000 that had over 30 Secure Communities submissions for the quarter), and 5 smaller jurisdictions (those with populations under 100,000) that produced the most anomalous results in the first phase of the analysis. CRCL stated that anomalies may indicate

---

[49]These materials are optional and provided free of charge, and are not required as part of state or local law enforcement training.

[50]To improve the reliability of its analyses, CRCL's statistical monitoring does not include jurisdictions that submit fewer than 30 Secure Communities matches per quarter. For the third quarter of fiscal year 2011, this resulted in excluding 101 jurisdictions (10 percent of all Secure Communities jurisdictions and 0.4 percent of the population in counties where Secure Communities is activated from CRCL's analyses).

that police engaged in racial profiling, but they may also reflect local crime patterns and legitimate police practices. For example, they said, in a jurisdiction where highway patrol is a primary function, officers would be making more traffic stops, and higher rates of traffic offenses might be expected. According to CRCL, because its second-phase analysis relies in part on data collected by local and state law enforcement agencies, the data are frequently less consistent across jurisdictions. These variations present challenges for CRCL's analysis.

In the third phase, CRCL, in conjunction with ICE, plans to conduct inquiries into relevant policing practices in jurisdictions where the in-depth statistical analyses were unable to account for the anomalies in the statistical results.[51] Officials said the decision to proceed with the third phase of monitoring will be made on a case-by-case basis, and could, among other things, involve interviewing law enforcement personnel or complainants, or requesting documents from a law enforcement agency. ICE and CRCL officials said they would decide what actions they may take at the conclusion of the inquiry phase.

CRCL had planned to begin reporting the results of its statistical monitoring beginning with data from early fiscal year 2011, but began with the third quarter of fiscal year 2011. As of May 2012, CRCL was completing its analysis under the second phase for the third and fourth quarters of 2011. CRCL said the work and report have not yet been completed because of challenges with using multiple sources of data that were not designed for real-time monitoring. Examples of the data limitations and how CRCL plans to take the limitations into account in their analysis include the following:

- The FBI's Uniform Crime Reporting (UCR) Program summary reporting system (a FBI national crime database that includes the number and types of arrests by police department) is used by CRCL for its foreign-born arrest charge comparisons. However, participation in the UCR Program is voluntary and not all police departments in the United States participate, including, for example, 21 counties in Illinois. In such cases, CRCL plans to identify and use other data, such as the National Incident-Based Reporting System (NIBRS),

---

[51]CRCL also refers to this phase as "non-statistical review" because the term "investigation" may be misinterpreted as more comprehensive than what is actually involved.

another FBI UCR Program method for collecting crime data, and arrest data, if available, that are publicly reported outside the summary UCR system, by some states, such as Florida, through its state UCR program.

- There is a lag between the time that the U.S. Census Bureau's American Community Survey collects and releases demographic information on the foreign-born population in the United States. CRCL began working with the Community Survey data for the 2005-2009 period, and shifted to the 2006-2010 data when it became available in December 2011.

- Noncitizens in different parts of the country have different rates of inclusion in the IDENT database, making careful comparisons important and more difficult. Foreign-born residents who have not interacted with federal immigration agencies would not have been included in the IDENT database. The CRCL monitoring statistics could underestimate potential civil rights abuses in such jurisdictions, compared with jurisdictions in which IDENT includes a larger proportion of the foreign-born population. ICE stated that officials are working to better understand variation in IDENT coverage for improved comparisons.

- CRCL officials also said that in working with the actual arrest data for the first time, they are discovering and resolving such data problems as incongruous categorizations of crimes. For example, definitions of "serious" or "aggravated" arrests vary between the UCR and LESC. Consequently, CRCL's work with the first data set to account for such differences is taking longer than subsequent analysis is expected to take.

ICE, CRCL, and DHS headquarters officials met in May 2012 to assess the progress of the statistical monitoring effort, discuss potential changes to Secure Communities protocols as a result of the statistical analyses, determine what and how information from the monitoring effort will be reported, and decide on any actions to be taken at the conclusion of all monitoring phases. They determined that further development and analysis were required, and CRCL officials told us that follow-up sessions were scheduled for July 2012. CRCL officials explained that CRCL would issue its report when it is confident that everything possible had been done to resolve the statistical anomalies, because doing so would avoid inappropriately flagging jurisdictions whose statistics appeared anomalous, but were later explained. Once the first report is issued, according to CRCL officials, they expect to report quarterly.

Allegations of Civil Rights Abuses under Secure Communities Are Investigated under DHS's Complaint Process

Under a complaint process applicable to all of DHS, CRCL has opened four investigations, all in fiscal year 2011, of civil rights complaints that CRCL identified as involving Secure Communities. CRCL has authority to review and assess civil rights or civil liberties complaints regarding DHS policies, activities, or actions taken by DHS personnel, and receives complaints submitted by mail, e-mail, fax, and the CRCL telephone hotline.[52] CRCL also reviews a monthly list of complaints processed through the Joint Intake Center, and a complaint form is posted on the Secure Communities' and CRCL's websites.[53] CRCL officials stated they meet quarterly with community organizations and ask for allegations regarding Secure Communities to be forwarded.

ICE and CRCL issued a joint memorandum on June 14, 2011, outlining how civil rights complaints involving state and local law enforcement and Secure Communities would be addressed.[54] The memorandum noted that the strategy for Secure Communities differs from those of most other programs in that CRCL has no compulsory process that requires state and local LEAs to cooperate in CRCL investigations because CRCL and the LEAs do not have formal partnerships under Secure Communities. The memorandum stated that CRCL may initiate investigations based on complaints alleging misconduct, statistical information indicating anomalies in arrests that led to Secure Communities matches, or the results of third-party research. The investigation process can vary based on how the complaint was initiated and is described in the June memorandum.

---

[52]This authority is based on 6 U.S.C., §345(a)(1),(4) and (6); and 42 U.S.C. §2000ee-1(a)(2).

[53]The number of complaints on the monthly list varies, for example, from 27 in December 2011, to 64 in February 2012. The Joint Intake Center receives complaints from a variety of sources, and CRCL cannot identify whether a particular complaint call was based on the detainer form notice.

[54]Secure Communities complaints related to alleged misconduct of ICE contractors or employees are handled using standard procedures by ICE's Office of Professional Responsibility.

CRCL categorizes complaints by issue (what the complaint is about) and by the situation in which the issue occurred. There are 21 categories of issues, such as use of excessive force, sexual assault, or abuse, and 16 categories of situations, such as a complaint arising from a port of entry incident or a Secure Communities encounter. Knowing whether a complaint is actually related to Secure Communities is not always clear, CRCL officials stated. This is because not all of those who file complaints know that they were identified through Secure Communities, and conversely, some may mistakenly believe that Secure Communities was involved in their arrest when they were actually identified by other means. CRCL staff said they discuss each allegation to determine if it is related to Secure Communities by looking at the specifics of the complaint. CRCL officials said that under Secure Communities, likely complaint issues are those involving discrimination or profiling, Fourth Amendment rights, and language access issues.[55] A CRCL Complaint Opening Meeting group, composed of CRCL management, including the Compliance Branch Deputy Director and other stakeholders, decides on a weekly basis whether to take further action on specific complaints, using their professional judgment.[56]

Four investigations have been initiated by CRCL based on complaints regarding Secure Communities, three of which were submitted by one nongovernmental organization in one region. The complaints involve allegations that each of the four arrests was made because the officers believed the individuals were in the country illegally, and the individuals were arrested to determine their immigration status.

CRCL's Compliance Branch Director said there is no "standard" investigation process for a complaint because each complaint is fact specific; but, in each case, CRCL requests documents from ICE and the local law enforcement agency that arrested the complainant. If available, the complainant is interviewed, in addition to relevant DHS personnel and witnesses. CRCL officials stated that CRCL is currently working through

---

[55]Fourth Amendment rights relate to the part of the Bill of Rights that guards against unreasonable searches and seizures (including arrests), along with requiring any arrest or search warrant to be judicially sanctioned and supported by probable cause. See U.S. Const. amend IV.

[56]CRCL may not initiate an investigation if the DHS Inspector General decides to investigate. All matters are first referred to the Inspector General for investigation, and if the Inspector General declines to investigate, the matter is referred back to CRCL.

procedures for investigating Secure Communities complaints with two local law enforcement agencies and requested that officers sit for voluntary interviews. These complaints are taking longer than what is normal for investigations of DHS policy and practices, officials said, in part because of the need to create new procedures with local law enforcement for investigating the allegations.

Conclusions

In 2009, about 11.5 million noncitizens were living in the United States without lawful immigration status, some of whom have been arrested and convicted of various crimes and incarcerated. Secure Communities assists in identifying those who have been incarcerated and are subject to removal. ICE has invested millions of dollars to modernize ACRIMe capabilities that are central to Secure Communities' success, but has not followed best practices in its acquisition of the modernized technology. Effective management of future ACRIMe modernization efforts hinges on establishing well-defined requirements and the development of a reliable integrated master schedule. Likewise, a modernized ACRIMe, along with the extension of Secure Communities to all jurisdictions, will change ICE workforce requirements for the analysis of immigration status determinations. Developing a workforce plan to guide workforce resource decisions could help ensure workforce decisions are made in an effective and cost-efficient manner.

Recommendations for Executive Action

To help ensure that ICE acquires effective technology to support the Secure Communities program and effectively uses its workforce, we recommend that the Director of ICE take the following three actions to follow sound management practices:

- establish well-defined requirements prior to awarding additional ACRIMe modernization contracts;

- develop an integrated master schedule that identifies all tasks to be performed by the government and current and future contractors, and links activities being performed by different contractors; and

- develop a workforce plan to support the analysis of immigration status determinations under Secure Communities.

Agency Comments and GAO's Evaluation

We provided a draft of this report to DHS and DOJ for their review and comment. DHS provided written comments which are reprinted in full in Appendix II. DHS concurred with our three recommendations and described efforts underway to address them. For example, with respect to establishing well-defined requirements prior to awarding additional ACRIMe modernization contracts, DHS stated that ICE is piloting an incremental development and requirements definition process within ACRIMe, including using smaller requirements teams to complete requirements by the end of July 2012, before additional contracts are issued. These actions are consistent with the intent of the recommendation and should help ICE manage future ACRIMe modernization efforts. With respect to developing an integrated master schedule, DHS reiterated that it began developing such a schedule in April 2012 and expects to complete it by the end of December 2012. This action is consistent with the intent of the recommendation and should improve ICE's understanding of how schedule changes in individual contracts may affect the overall modernization effort. With respect to developing a workforce plan, DHS noted that ICE plans to complete a proposal for consolidating Interoperability Response Centers into one central location by the end of December 2012. DHS stated that it will determine what, if any, additional workforce plans are needed after it completes the proposal. While this is a step in the right direction, we continue to believe that ICE would benefit from comprehensive workforce planning that includes examining how to reduce the existing duplication of effort between LESC and ICE field offices when ICE deploys modernized ACRIMe. DHS also provided technical comments, which we incorporated as appropriate.

DOJ did not have formal comments on our draft report, but provided technical comments, which we incorporated as appropriate.

As agreed with your office, unless you publicly announce the contents of this report earlier, we plan no further distribution until 30 days from the report date. At that time, we will send copies to the Secretary of the Department of Homeland Security and other interested parties. In addition, the report will be available at no charge on the GAO website at http://www.gao.gov.

If you or your staff have any questions about this report, please contact me at (202) 512-8777 or gamblerr@gao.gov. Contact points for our Offices of Congressional Relations and Public Affairs may be found on the last page of this report. Key contributors to this report are listed in appendix III.

Sincerely yours,

Rebecca Gambler
Acting Director
Homeland Security and Justice Issues

Appendix I: Alien Criminal Response Information Management Modernization Contracts

As of April 2012, the U.S. Immigration and Customs Enforcement (ICE) had awarded four contracts and planned to award additional contracts to modernize its Alien Criminal Response Information Management (ACRIMe) system. In commenting on a draft of this report, in June 2012 ICE officials told us that they now plan to award three new contracts and that the work for the previously planned ACRIMe/ENFORCE Integration and Batch Processing contracts would be incorporated into other ACRIMe modernization efforts.[1] Table 6 provides summary information on these contracts as of April 2012.

Table 6: ACRIMe Modernization Contracts

Dollars in millions

Contract	Description	Contract period	Estimated deployment as of April 2012[a]	Contract value as of April 2012[b]	Funding as of April 2012
ACRIMe-1[c]	To develop a modernized ACRIMe system for accessing multiple law enforcement and immigration databases	June 2008-May 2012[d]	Canceled	$12.0 (actual)	$12.0
Automated Threat Prioritization (ATP)	To allow modernized ACRIMe users to automatically retrieve prior conviction information from state and federal criminal history records	September 2009-August 2014	December 2012	26.1 (ICE estimate)	21.5
Status Determination Support (SDS)	To develop five web services to enhance modernized ACRIMe's capability to determine immigration status: • Status Determination Support • Automated National Crime Information Center (NCIC) Warrants • Criminal Alien Tracking • Jail Roster/Release Tracking • Integrated Case Management	September 2009-August 2014[e]	Canceled	14.3 (actual)	14.3

[1]We will continue to monitor these efforts as part of our recommendation follow-up work.

Dollars in millions

Contract	Description	Contract period	Estimated deployment as of April 2012[a]	Contract value as of April 2012[b]	Funding as of April 2012
ACRIMe-2	To complete the development of the modernized ACRIMe system that had been developed under the ACRIMe-1 contract and provide ongoing operations and maintenance support	September 2011-August 2016	July 2012[f]	8.1 (ICE estimate)	2.3
NCIC Wants and Warrants	To develop the service for processing NCIC warrants that ICE originally planned to develop in the SDS contract	ICE plans to award the contract by the end of September 2012.	March 2013	1.7 (ICE estimate)	0
Communications Center	To develop call center capability within the modernized ACRIMe system that ICE originally planned to develop with the ACRIMe-1 contract	ICE plans to award the contract by the end of September 2012.	March 2013	1.7 (ICE estimate)	0
External Search Service	To develop the status determination support service to search multiple databases that ICE originally planned to develop with the SDS contract	ICE plans to award the contract by the end of December 2012.	June 2013	1.1 (ICE estimate)	0
ACRIMe/ ENFORCE Integration[g]	To develop the integrated case management that ICE originally planned to develop with the SDS contract to allow modernized ACRIMe users to automatically export data into ENFORCE	ICE plans to award the contract by the end of December 2012.	June 2013	2.3 (ICE estimate)	0
Batch Processing[h]	To develop the service for jail roster/release tracking service that ICE originally planned to develop with the SDS contract	ICE plans to award the contract by the end of December 2012.	June 2013	$.3 (ICE estimate)	0

Source: GAO analysis of ICE information.

[a]The deployment dates are the dates for the initial operational capability, rather than the final operational capability. ICE is using an iterative approach, and officials expect that some additional work will be needed after the initial deployment before the technology is fully functional.

[b]For the two contracts that were canceled (ACRIME-1 and SDS), the contract value is equal to the total amount ICE spent on the contract. For the other two contracts that have been awarded (ATP and ACRIMe-2), the source of the estimated contract value is the most recent contract modification as of April 2012. For the remaining five contracts that have not been awarded, ICE officials provided the estimates for the contracts' values.

cThe contract that ICE awarded in 2008 to acquire the modernized ACRIMe system was also to acquire other technology-related services. We use the term "ACRIMe-1" to refer to just the portion of the contract related to acquiring the modernized ACRIMe system.

dICE funded this contract through September 2011, since ICE decided not to continue using this contractor.

eICE canceled this contract in August 2011 because of delays with ACRIMe modernization.

fICE is incrementally deploying the modernized ACRIMe system. According to ICE, in February 2012, a version of the modernized ACRIMe system that could search the Federal Bureau of Investigation's National Crime Information Center was deployed in the Law Enforcement Support Center. However, the system will not be able to process requests for immigration status determinations until July 2012, when ICE plans to deploy an updated modernized ACRIMe system to the Law Enforcement Support Center. ICE plans to deploy the modernized ACRIMe system with immigration status determination functionality across ICE in December 2012.

gENFORCE is a database that maintains information related to the investigation, arrest, booking, detention, and removal or persons encountered during immigration investigations and operations conducted by ICE and U.S. Customs and Border Protection. In commenting on a draft of this report, in June 2012 ICE officials told us the work for the previously planned ACRIMe/ENFORCE Integration contract would be incorporated into other ACRIMe modernization efforts. We will continue to monitor these efforts as part of our recommendation follow-up work.

hIn commenting on a draft of this report, in June 2012 ICE officials told us the work for Batch Processing contract would be incorporated into other ACRIMe modernization efforts. We will continue to monitor these efforts as part of our recommendation follow-up work.

Appendix II: Comments from the Department of Homeland Security

U.S. Department of Homeland Security
Washington, DC 20528

July 3, 2012

Rebecca Gambler
Acting Director, Homeland Security and Justice
U.S. Government Accountability Office
441 G Street, NW
Washington, DC 20548

Re: Draft Report GAO-12-708, "SECURE COMMUNITIES: Criminal Alien Removals
Increased, but Better Technology Planning Needed"

Dear Ms. Gambler:

Thank you for the opportunity to review and comment on this draft report. The U.S. Department
of Homeland Security (DHS) appreciates the U.S. Government Accountability Office's (GAO's)
work in planning and conducting its review and issuing this report.

DHS is pleased to note GAO's positive recognition of the Department's efforts to focus on
identifying potentially removable national security and public safety threats, including criminal
aliens in state and local law enforcement custody. U.S. Immigration Customs and Enforcement
(ICE) remains committed to adhering to best practices in acquiring Secure Communities-related
technology and safeguarding and protecting civil rights and liberties under the Secure
Communities program.

The draft report contained three recommendations with which the Department concurs.
Specifically, GAO recommended to the Director of ICE:

Recommendation 1: Establish well-defined requirements prior to awarding additional ACRIMe
modernization contracts.

Response: Concur. ICE will ensure that well-defined requirements will be available during the
development phase, prior to awarding contracts, and throughout development. ICE is currently
piloting an incremental development and requirements definition process within the Alien
Criminal Response Information Management System (ACRIMe) project. As part of this project, the
ICE Office of the Chief Information Officer (OCIO) is now developing smaller requirements
teams to complete the requirements definition process before contracts are issued for design and
development services. These requirements teams work with government program managers,

1

business owners and system users to thoroughly understand current and future processes and ensure those processes are captured in requirements models that may be used in the development process. When the development teams are contracted, the requirements teams regularly interact with them to ensure understanding. In addition, the development teams have transitioned from the use of historical "waterfall" development processes to the use of an "agile" process, which permits development teams to focus on and release pieces of functionality to the users as they are created, rather than having to wait for the entire system to be developed. As a result, ICE will be involved throughout the development by providing feedback to developers at regular intervals in order to increase the quality and responsiveness of the system. Estimated Completion Date (ECD): July 31, 2012.

Recommendation 2: Develop an integrated master schedule that identifies all tasks to be performed by the government and current and future contractors, and links activities being performed by different contractors.

Response: Concur. As the report notes, ICE OCIO began developing an integrated master schedule (IMS) in April 2012. This integrated schedule provides all known contractor and government tasks necessary to complete each of the individual projects in the Criminal Alien Identification Initiative (CAII) portfolio. Tasks for contracts that have not yet been awarded are not yet included in the IMS, but anticipated release dates based on the CAII Product Roadmap have been included. The CAII Product Roadmap is a joint document created by the CAII Program Manager and the Secure Communities Product Owner that maps each of the high-level business requirements to specific pieces of system capabilities, allowing the Program Manager and Product Owner to prioritize the development of the capabilities into a release timeline. The release timeline takes into account time required to ensure that user and system requirements are well defined, procurement lead time, and the level of effort needed to develop the capabilities. In addition, beginning in July 2012, contractor teams and government personnel involved in the CAII effort will begin having regular meetings to review the impacts of scheduled events and future schedule-related risks. ECD: December 31, 2012.

Recommendation 3: Develop a workforce plan to support the analysis of immigration status determinations under Secure Communities.

Response: Concur. As GAO alluded to in its report, detailed workforce plans regarding personnel allocations at the Law Enforcement Support Center (LESC), Interoperability Response Centers, and ICE Enforcement and Removal Operations (ERO) Field Offices are informed by the analysis of the operational impact of deployment of the modernized ACRIMe system.

ICE is currently developing a proposal for the consolidation of the Interoperability Response Centers in anticipation of the nationwide deployment of Secure Communities' use of Automated Biometric Identification System (IDENT)/Integrated Automated Fingerprint Identification System (IAFIS) interoperability and the modernized ACRIMe system. The proposal will detail

2

the proposed consolidation of the Los Angeles, Buffalo, Miami, and Chicago Interoperability Response Centers into one central location, and standardization of processes at the central location and the LESC in an effort to better support the analysis of immigration status determinations under Secure Communities. We estimate this proposal will be completed by December 31, 2012, after which, we will determine what additional workforce plans are needed, if any, as appropriate.

Again, thank you for the opportunity to review and comment on this draft report. Technical comments were previously provided under separate cover. Please feel free to contact me if you have any questions. We look forward to working with you in the future.

Sincerely,

Jim H. Crumpacker
Director
Departmental GAO-OIG Liaison Office

3

Appendix III: GAO Contacts and Staff Acknowledgments

GAO Contact	Rebecca Gambler, (202) 512-8777 or gamblerr@gao.gov
Staff Acknowledgments	In addition to the contact named above, Evi Rezmovic (Assistant Director), David Alexander, Frances Cook, Kevin Craw, Dorian Dunbar, Monica Kelly, Jason Lee, Heather May, Linda Miller, Karen Richey, and Nate Tranquilli made key contributions to this report.